The Eight-Step Mu......

Learning and Teaching with a Smile!

Festus E. Obiakor, Ph.D.
Emporia State University

Gwen! Personal Copy! Keep!!. I've seen you grow, you're amazing! I'm glad to know you!! Festus.

KENDALL/HUNT PUBLISHING COMPANY
4050 Westmark Drive   Dubuque, Iowa 52002

This edition has been printed directly from camera-ready copy.

Copyright © 1994 by Kendall/Hunt Publishing Company

ISBN 0-8403-9801-8

Printed in the United States of America
10 9 8 7 6 5 4 3 2 1

Foreword

Public discourse on multicultural education has centered on definition, pedagogy, curricula, or program implementation. Very little has been written about the philosophical benefits and behavioral linkages gained from the effects of multiculturalism on learning. This book responds to that need. It examines multicultural education from a practical, logistical point-of-view. This book is organized according to key concepts essential to understanding and practicing multicultural teaching. Dr. Obiakor, through his analogies and personal recollections, provides a step-by-step approach to bridging the gap between traditional teaching philosophies and the implementation of multicultural teaching practices. Each step introduces the reader to beginning applications for multicultural learning and equips both the neophyte and seasoned educator with basic principles for teaching and implementing multicultural curricula.

In Step One, "Know Who You Are," Dr. Obiakor presents the foundation upon which strong pedagogy is developed. He illustrates how personal strength and confidence enhances an educator's ability to teach with confidence and conviction. Developing an appreciation of and acceptance for human diversity in others enables the effective educator to teach without biases. In Step Two, "When in Doubt, Learn the Facts," Dr. Obiakor beautifully defines the dynamics of multiculturalism. This chapter projects the richness of a heterogeneous society and the role of the educator in advancing such a society. Dr. Obiakor's discussions of myths and controversy surrounding multicultural education not only challenge the educators' readiness for the classroom but makes a strong case for its universal inclusion. In Step Three, "Change Your Thinking," Dr. Obiakor deals with re-orienting educators' thinking and behavioral practices. This step examines the effects of one's value system and perceived stereotypes upon teaching behaviors within the classroom. More importantly, Dr. Obiakor tells us that change begins from within ourselves and that respect and appreciation for different cultures are mandatory if educators are to teach inclusively and promote human dignity within the classroom.

In Step Four, "Use Resource Persons," Dr. Obiakor demonstrates the need for diverse role models, the effective use of community resources, and the need for progressive, collaborative efforts between professionals and paraprofessionals in order for multicultural learning and teaching to occur and to proceed with longevity. Dr. Obiakor provides illustrative examples of how professionals and paraprofessionals can work together to enhance

i

multiculturalism within the classroom. In Step Five, "Build Self-Concepts," Dr. Obiakor reiterates that self-concept is not predetermined and that educators can use various methods of instruction to enhance self-concept. He points out that many educators are sometimes unaware of their influence upon self-concept in student learners and are ill-equipped to face the challenges posed by non-traditional students. In the multicultural classroom, educators respond individually and collectively to all students and capitalize upon cultural contributions and heritage. Dr. Obiakor identifies listening and observation as key attributes for strengthening multicultural teaching and learning.

In Step Six, "Teach with Divergent Techniques," Dr. Obiakor uses excerpts, case examples, and tailored instructional practices to demonstrate important heterogenous teaching principles. He outlines six theoretical models that reflect divergent orientations appropriate for use in the multicultural classroom. Through his definitions of educator role and preparedness, Dr. Obiakor successfully addresses the necessity of teachers borrowing from other disciplines to reach their highest levels of learning. It is this learning that turns good teachers into great teachers. In Step Seven, "Make the Right Choices," Dr. Obiakor discusses the six theoretical models from Step Six, focusing upon the need to make good decisions, and detailing how sound decision-making impacts cooperative learning and teaching in the multicultural classroom. Choices, according to Dr. Obiakor, influence actions. The right choice provides opportunity and creates a nurturing, learning environment. In Step Eight, "Continue to Learn," Dr. Obiakor discusses how inappropriate perceptions and presumptions about minority groups lead to dehumanizing values and behaviors towards these groups. The consequences of social systems' failure to respond to multiculturalism is exemplified in Dr. Obiakor's portrayal of a monocultural society. He details a multicultural learning process and illustrates how educators may become role models for that which they need to exemplify.

Dr. Obiakor approaches the reader as an agent of change. He speaks in jargon-free language, using analogies and personal illustrations to aid understanding. A running abstract with common characters introduces the theme for each step, relating its content to real-life applications. On occasion, Dr. Obiakor asks us to reflect inwardly as he guides us through cultural sensitive behaviors. In these instances, he suggests that the reader considers how his [Dr. Obiakor] material relates to personal experiences, and prescribes meaningful activities that help the reader solidify understanding of multiculturalism or redefine the meaning of success.

Multicultural learning is an interesting, exciting, and at times, humorous process. It is also the process that will create a partnership between society, politics, and economics. The importance of this partnership will be felt as the reader journeys through this powerful, and much needed book. I highly recommend this book to undergraduate and graduate students, general and special educators, service providers and parents, and community and business leaders.

Narviar Cathcart Barker, Ph.D.
Georgia State University
February 1994

Preface

One fundamental issue confronting educators, service providers and society today is how to infuse multicultural learning and teaching into the general frame of activities. The mere mention of multicultural education opens up a dreaded "can of worms," yet everyone I have talked to believes "racism" is repugnant. Frequently, the politics of multicultural education masquerades the appreciation and wonder that diversity brings to the classroom.

The old adage "two heads are better than one" comes to be appreciated as we talk about multiculturalism. Multicultural education is an addition to (rather than a subtraction from) the education that exists today. This, of course, is the book's major thrust, but, how best to achieve this goal became my major challenge. The best ways I thought were to add personal flavors to a complex issue and to make use of extensive workshops and seminars I have conducted for school and university systems. To a large extent, I have been able to achieve my goal.

This has been a fun book to write. In the end, I am sure classroom teachers, service providers, researchers, scholars, consultants, parents and students of all races and creeds will find it beneficial. This book should be a catharsis for all of us and something we can learn from.

Books of this nature would be impossible without the support of family, friends, and colleagues. My special thanks go to Bob Algozzine, Dorothy Aramburo, Alfredo Artiles, Leonard Baca, Chiquita Ballenger, Narviar Cathcart Barker, Helen Bessant-Byrd, David Byrne, Steve Davis, Doris Duncan, Bridgie Ford, Rodney Fowler, Mary Franklin, Anne Gallegos, Robert Glennen, Carolyn Golightly, Eileen Goor, Mark Goor, Cassondria Greene, Lori Grilliot, Pauline Harris-Obiakor, Asa Hilliard, Barbara Holder, Mike Kelly, Gregory Maltby, Tes Mehring, Douglas Muller, Charles Chidi Obiakor, Gina Chioma Obiakor, Kristen Ego Obiakor, John Ogbu, Blair Olson, Lee Owens, James Patton, David Payne, Loretta Prater, Carolyn Princes, John Rahija, Bruce Ramirez, Bill Samuelson, Paula Sauder, Judy Schwenn, Jack Skillett, Fred Spooner, Steve Stile, Beverly Thompson, Stanley Trent, Faye Vowell, Charles Weiner, David Weintraub, Bill Yates, and Naomi Zigmond. My colleagues and students at Emporia State University have proven once more that one does not have to be a minority to accept and value multicultural learning and teaching. I am especially grateful to John Schwenn and Kenneth Weaver for their helpful comments and suggestions in the initial draft of this work. Finally, I want to thank Geri Krier and the Word Processing staff of the Teachers College, Emporia State University for typing the manuscript.

Festus E. Obiakor

This book is dedicated to:

Teachers/Professors who believe in their students;
Service providers/Professionals who believe in their students;
Parents/Guardians who believe in their children;
Community/Business leaders who believe in their children.

TABLE OF CONTENTS

Foreword   i

Preface   iv

STEP ONE: Know Who You Are   1

STEP TWO: When in Doubt, Learn the Facts   6

STEP THREE: Change Your Thinking   14

STEP FOUR: Use Resource Persons   22

STEP FIVE: Build Self-Concepts   34

STEP SIX: Teach with Divergent Techniques   46

STEP SEVEN: Make the Right Choices   62

STEP EIGHT: Continue to Learn   75

Afterword   94

References   102

STEP ONE

Know Who You Are

We gain knowledge of ourselves by identifying ourselves with others, but that is not enough--that only gives us the fantasies of sex and the parodies of power, the absurd strutting daydreams of Secret Agent 007 and Butterfield 8. We must enter others in order to share their conflicts, in order that we shall feel in their lives what we know in our own: the human dilemma. The knowledge of self cannot be formalized because it cannot be closed, even provisionally; it is perpetually open, because the dilemma is perpetually unresolved. (Bronowski, 1971, pp. 136-137)

Race, color, and tribalization have continued to matter in today's educational programs. In the face of these challenges, I have refused to be negative and presumptuous. I strongly believe when we get angry, we fail to empower ourselves and lose focus on our goals and objectives in life. Implicitly and explicitly, my interactions with people around me have strengthened my metamorphoses into a "whole" person. It is immoral for me to deny who I am or apologize for who I am. I have experienced racism in different fashions; and as a Black man, I have been tempted to believe the conspiracy theory and/or the permanence of racism. However, my *wonderful* relationships with different people have convinced me that *anger* or *presumption* is not the solution. I am more convinced than before that the real antidote to racism is our willingness to engage in multicultural learning and teaching at all facets of our society.

As a United States citizen who immigrated from Nigeria in West Africa to study and work, multicultural teaching has become an almost daily occurrence. The older I get, the more exciting and humorous is my teaching. Most people take life too seriously and this seriousness frequently masquerades their judgements. I still remember going to an elementary school to speak to students about African cultures. I wore an expensive three piece French suit to do this presentation. In the middle of my speech, one student raised his hand with a simple but thought-provoking question: "Where is the African?" I replied: "I am the African." It was very difficult to convince these students even though my accent was very revealing. To them, my accent did not (and should not) make me an African. In their opinion, I did not look like an African. They noted that I did not fit the image of what they were told by their teacher and what they read from their books and saw on television. These students had been told that Africans live in huts and dance naked around drums with their spears as they celebrate after hunting. I was reminded of those Tarzan movies where the White man's bravery and gallantry markedly contrasted with Africans' helplessness. I was in a quandary and forced to search my soul for some important questions. "Should I discredit these students' teacher? Should I be upset at the teacher who invited me?" The students saw that I was dumbfounded. One of them asserted: "Maybe you were born in America but grew up in Nigeria." I responded again: "I am from Nigeria in Africa--Africans come in different forms."

My discussions with these young students have several educational implications. First, we clearly must change our thinking and desist from judging without knowledge. Second, little learning is a dangerous thing; when drunk deep, it sobers the learner. So, when in doubt, people must learn the facts. Third, resource persons must be used to reduce misconceptions. Fourth, since children can teach adults some lessons--let's let them teach and build their self-concepts. Fifth, different techniques work in different situations. Sixth, people must never stop learning--education is a continuous process of growth.

My accent frequently gives me away. I have been asked many interesting questions about my place of origin; my answers have been interesting but educational. I will recount a few. On the question, "Do you know Chidi Okeke [a fictitious name]? I went to school with him. He is from Africa." My response usually is, "Do you know Judy Jones [a fictitious name]? I met her in Fort Worth, Texas." On the question, "Do you have roads in Africa?" My response to the question usually depends on my mood. When I am in a happy mood, my response is, "Yes, we have roads like the ones in Arkansas, Mississippi, Tennessee, etc." When I am in a humorous mood, my response is, "No, we live in the jungle." On the question, "Do you have houses in Africa?" My response is, "No, we have only one house, that is, the American Embassy." On the question, "Do you drink coffee or tea in Africa?" My response is, "No, we drink blood." On the question, "When did you start speaking English?" My response is, "In the plane." The statement that follows this response is fascinating. "You must be very smart." And I follow with "Thank you for your honor." On the question, "When did you learn to dress the way you do?" My response is, "Last month" depending on when I was asked the question. The most interesting question came from a former colleague (a university professor of a special education department) who asked, "Have you ever thought about going to a speech and language pathologist because of your accent?" To this question, my answer was just a smile.

These questions and answers are samples, but they confirm the need for multicultural teaching and global education. Lest I forget, Africa is three times the size of the United States. Nigeria is an European colonized country of about 120 million people living in 30 states of the federation. It is a Commonwealth nation with English as its "lingua franca." In other words, Nigerians have divergent cultures and dialects, but when they meet, their language of communication is English. Nigeria is the seventh largest exporter of oil to the United States and imports goods and technical know-how from the United States. As interrelated as Nigeria and the United States are, there still exists the gross lack of knowledge about Nigeria by many Americans. The whole world is interdependent. For further reading, see Dr. Ezekiel Mphahlele's 1974 book, *The African Image* and Dr. A. Babs Fafunwa's 1976 book, *New Perspectives in African Education.* In addition, read Obiakor and Maltby's 1989 book, *Pragmatism and Education in Africa.*

The mere mention of multicultural education chills conversation. Let's not deceive ourselves, everyone has some form of prejudice that comes in many modes, i.e., the kind of individuals or groups we like to fraternize with, the kind of food we like to eat, the kind of clothes we like to wear, the kind of places we like to visit, the kind of schools we like to attend, etc. In the same vein, we have some form of relationship with other people different from ourselves. We live in a global community whether we accept it or not, yet, we are frequently scared of the unknown. There are universal values that permeate all cultures. For example, there is a reward for good deeds and punishment for bad deeds, inspite of one's culture, society or nation. Invariably, the issue of what is "good" or "bad" is dependent on culture or society. We tend to be classically conditioned to believe what we believe. Anything new disrupts our fragile equilibrium.

I still remember landing at John F. Kennedy (JFK) airport the first time I arrived in the United States. What a joy it was to finally arrive in this great country, a dream for many individuals! My next flight was supposed to take off at LaGuardia airport. I was glad to find a taxi from JFK airport to LaGuardia. I was also glad to find a driver and two White men already in the cab. Since I did not know where LaGuardia airport was, I had to rely on the driver (a White man) and the other two White passengers. As we approached LaGuardia airport, the driver suddenly stopped. These men robbed me of all the money I had to survive in America. They forced me at gun-point to sign all my travellers' checks. I begged them not to kill me. They did not kill me but they left me penniless. I did not tell the Nigerian and American Embassies because I did not want this incident to be sensationalized by the news media. I finally arrived at my destination and related my experience to the International Student Advisor (a White man) who immediately helped me to get an on-campus job. On this predominantly White campus, I met many wonderful professors and students who had similar beliefs and values with me, their race and national origin notwithstanding.

A few lessons can be learned from these "bad" and "good" encounters. First, perceptions are deceptive. Second, generalizations are dangerous. Third, human-beings (even those of the same race) differ within and between themselves. Fourth, teachings, based on classical conditioning (with no disrespect for Ivan Pavlov), can be wrong. Fifth, I have learned to be much more careful when I travel to unfamiliar destinations. Sixth, life is full of good and bad experiences, and we can learn from them. With respect to multicultural education, some questions deserve to be asked. Should I be scared of all White people because I was robbed by three marauders who happened to be White men in LaGuardia, New York? Should I assume that all White men are senseless thieves? I do not think so. These kinds of thinking would have narrowed my options in life. Many of my role models and mentors are White men and women as well as African-Americans, Hispanic-Americans, Native-Americans, and Asian-Americans. It is interesting to note that in my young career I have touched many lives. This is why I suggest we must know who we are and who others are in order to enjoy the diversities of life. In other words, we must be ready for shifts in power (see Alvin Toffler's 1991 book, *Powershift*).

Today, many educators seem to be classically conditioned. They refuse to try something "new" because the "old" technique seems to be yielding dividends. This trend has been evident in general and special education. It is no wonder terms like integration, inclusion, collaboration, consultation and multiculturalism have come to play in today's school systems and general and special classroom instructions. It is amazing, however, that when we feel good about people around us, we tend to (a) integrate their ideas into our ideas, (b) include them in our day-to-day activities, (c) collaborate with them, (d) consult and counsel with them when necessary, and (e) appreciate their different beliefs. For further information, read Drs. Alba Ortiz and Bruce Ramirez's 1989 book, *School and the Culturally Diverse Exceptional Student*. Additionally, read Drs. Donald Atkinson, George Morten and Derald Wing

Sue's 1993 book, *Counseling American Minorities: A Cross-Cultural Perspective.*

In summary, the major goal of this text is to help us to feel good about multicultural education. I intend to address in many ways our conceptions and misconceptions about enjoying the diversities of life. We should all imagine how boring this life would be if we had one *skin color*, one *race*, one *gender*, one *religion*, one *language*, one *culture*, and one *nation*. Let me push it a little further! Think about how boring it would be if we all ate the same food, drove the same cars, wore the same clothes, built the same houses, danced to the same music, had the same kings and queens, lived in the same homes, etc. Our diversities have served us well. Let us enjoy and celebrate them with a smile!

STEP TWO

When in Doubt, Learn the Facts

We pass through this world but once. Few tragedies can be
more extensive than the stunting of life, few injustices deeper
than the denial of an opportunity to strive or even to hope, by a
limit imposed from without, but falsely identified as lying
within. (Gould, 1981, pp. 28-29)

Multiculturalism has become a catchword in today's society.
Elementary, middle school, high school, and college teachers have been
struggling with how best to incorporate multiculturalism into their
identification, assessment, placement and instructional processes. Most teachers
want to help diverse students to maximize their potential -- this frequently
results in a "rat-race" for quick fixes and easy solutions. A few years ago, the
American Association of Colleges for Teacher Education (AACTE) (1988)
reported in their book, *Minority Recruitment and Retention*, that:

1. Blacks represent 16.2% of the children in public schools, but
    only 6.9% of the teachers.
2. Hispanics represent 9.1% of the children in public schools,
    but only 1.9% of the teachers.
3. Asian/Pacific Islanders represent 2.5% of the children in
    public schools, but only 0.9% of the teachers.
4. American Indians/Alaskan Natives represent 0.9% of the children in
    public schools, but only 0.6% of the teachers.
5. Whites represent 71.2% of the children in public schools,
    but 89.6% of the teachers. (p. 15)

AACTE's data appear depressing. As we have seen, there are more
White teachers than minority teachers in our public schools. It stands to reason
that we need to educate White teachers on how to teach minority students.
Apparently, multicultural education ought to start in teacher education programs
already overburdened by state requirements (see Dr. Mary Dilworth's 1992
book, *Diversity in Teacher Education: New Expectations*). Students are
required to make passing scores in the Pre-Professional Skills Test (PPST) and
the National Teacher Examination (NTE) even when they maintain 2.5, or in
some cases, 2.75 (out of 4.0) grade point averages. Like most standardized

tests, they lack reliability and validity (Ysseldyke, Algozzine and Thurlow, 1992)--they seem to be culturally biased (Samuda and Lewis, 1992), yet we continue to use them. These tests have little or no correlation to teachers' abilities to teach and many minority students have consistently performed poorly on them. I do not think anyone can justify why we continue to use and interpret them the way we do.

In my years of college teaching, I have taught very few minority students in my education courses. It is always controversial to discuss multicultural issues, even though these students will confront multicultural issues as teachers in our public schools. Through the years, my students have informed me that some other professors downplay or fail to discuss multicultural education; and when they do, it is usually not detailed. Today, I am more convinced than ever that most students are willing to learn about multicultural education.

Sometimes I find myself as "the lonely bird in the desert." As a student, I was either the first Black, the first Black male, the only Black or the only Black male in my graduate programs. As a university professor, I have been either the first Black, the first Black male, the only Black or the only Black male in the teacher education program. I continuously encounter faculty and students who are decent individuals but not well-prepared for multicultural education in teacher education programs. This lack of preparation makes it almost unfair for teacher education graduates to engage in multicultural teaching. It is important we prepare all students for realities of life. We cannot continue to prepare students homogeneously for a very heterogeneous society. There is nothing wrong with the European culture which has permeated our educational systems. Similarly, there is nothing wrong with minority cultures which we are trying to incorporate into our educational systems. What is wrong today is the inability of schools and colleges to incorporate all cultures to give a balanced education to their students (see Dr. Vincent Parillo's 1980 book, *Strangers to These Shores*).

What, then, is culture? I define culture as a complex web which unites knowledge, beliefs, arts, morals, laws, customs, capabilities and habits acquired by an individual in the society. Put another way, we come from different cultures and feel proud to come from our respective cultures. We get very upset when people attempt to denigrate our cultures, yet American demographics are changing, and the American society likewise is changing. The dominance of one culture over another is like a wrestling match. The most powerful or skillful wrestler takes the opponent down; however, both wrestlers usually are down. The victor cannot brag that the defeated opponent has fallen because they are both down. When the victor stands up, the defeated opponent will stand up. Logically, it is self-destructive for one culture to assume dominance over other cultures. All cultures (including the dominant culture) are down when one culture is down. For further information, read Dr. Joe Feagin's 1978 book, *Racial and Ethnic Relations* and Dr. Arthur Schlesinger's 1992 book, *The Disuniting of America: Reflections of a Multicultural Society.*

Educational systems and societies progress when cultures interact with each other. I love country music--I am a great fan of Crystal Gayle, George Jones, Willie Nelson, Dolly Parton, Charlie Pride, Kenny Rogers, George Strait, Randy Travis, and Don Williams. Country music has always been popular in many African nations. My students, friends and colleagues sometimes find it surprising to believe. I love Hip-hop and Rap music because of the energy that they generate on young African-Americans. I love Reggae music because of its spirituality and songs of freedom. I have many White friends who love Reggae, Hip-hop and Rap music. In fact, one of them, a devout Mormon, is very fascinated with Hip-hop music. His usual question is, "Why can't good music be good music?" My usual response is, "What role does race have to play with music?" Surprisingly, to many Americans, racial lines are drawn on every activity. That is where the frustration and stress come in. I still remember visiting one of the leading chain stores to buy the Christmas album of Kenny Rogers and his son. A White lady saw me checking out the album--even though I was a stranger to her, she still had the audacity to question why a Black man should buy a country album. My response to her was simple: "Thank you, ma'am, I didn't know that Charlie Pride was White." For those who do not know, Charlie Pride is an African-American and a great country musician with a world-wide appeal. I have used music as an example because it exposes knowledge, language, beliefs, arts, customs, and habits--music videos can be very informative on cultural variables. We cannot afford to downplay or ignore them. The criticisms given to Rap and Hip-hop music today were similar to the ones given to Elvis Presley (the King of Rock N' Roll) when he joined those that introduced the Rock N' Roll culture some years ago.

As I indicated earlier, the mere mention of multicultural education breeds resentment and controversy. The following myths have been responsible for the resentment:

1. Multicultural education means that "quality" education will be dethroned.

2. Multicultural education is a racist fight to denigrate the already established Eurocentric education.

3. Multicultural education is another welfare program.

4. Multicultural education is an imposition on the dominant White culture.

5. Multicultural education is expensive--it will drain (or waste) precious resources.

In reality, multicultural education enhances quality education. I define quality education as maximum learning which exposes students to "all sides of the coin." Multicultural education is an additional education to the Eurocentric education--it does not call for the elimination or domination of any culture in the educational system. It calls for additional cultures to the system. In other words, it is a fight against racism (and not a racist fight). Multicultural education is not another welfare program--it is an education that would capitalize on the resources and endowments of all individuals. Multicultural education is not an imposition on the dominant White culture--it is a pragmatic appeal to look at what has made America the greatest democracy in the world. Multicultural education is not expensive--it is the most cost-effective way to tap human resources of all Americans. The United States has not been successful in tapping her human resources (see Dr. William E. Burghardt Du Bois' 1961 book, *The Souls of the Black Folk*). The 1992 riot in Los Angeles, California is a great reminder that many minorities are dissolute and that we need to prioritize our priorities as a nation. For further reading, see Drs. Reid Luhman and Stuart Gilman's 1980 book, *Race and Ethnic Relations: The Social and Political Experience of Minority Groups*. In addition, read Dr. Derrick Bell's 1985 book, *And We are not Saved* and his 1992 book, *Faces at the Bottom of the Well*.

I will continue to believe it is cost-effective to educate all Americans. According to Gollnich and Chinn (1990) in their book, *Multicultural Education in a Pluralistic Society*, this goal can be achieved through multicultural education. They wrote:

An overall goal of multicultural education is to help all students develop their potential for academic, social, and vocational success. Educational and vocational options should not be limited by sex, age, ethnicity, native language, religion, class, or exceptionality. Educators are given the responsibility to help students contribute to and benefit from our democratic society. Within our pluralistic society, multicultural education values the existing diversity, positively portrays that diversity, and uses that diversity in the development of effective instructional categories for students in the classroom. In addition, multicultural education should help students think critically about institutionalized racism, classism, and sexism. (p. iii)

Gollnich and Chinn's definition is comprehensive enough to reduce the tension present when multicultural education is mentioned. Many Americans have been consistently misidentified, misassessed, miscategorized and miseducated. Gollnich and Chinn confirmed that "throughout U.S. history, racial identification has been used by policy makers and much of the population to classify groups of people as inferior or superior to another racial group" (p. 85). Based on this historical misclassification and problems associated with it, scholars and educators are almost obsessed in their search for the "real" meaning of multiculturalism today. This obsession has elevated multiculturalism as an inevitable force worthy of complementing major theoretical frameworks like humanism, behaviorism and cognitive learning theory. As Pederson (1991) pointed out:

Multiculturalism is a pervasive force in modern society that acknowledges the complexity of culture. During the last 20 years, multiculuralism has become recognized as a powerful force, not just for understanding "exotic" groups but also for understanding ourselves and those with whom we work in a complicated social context. Multiculturalism has gained the status of a general theory, complementing other scientific theories to explain human behavior. (p. 6)

Dr. John Ogbu (my tribesman, friend, renowned theorist and professor at the University of California at Berkeley, California) in his works has continuously indicated that minority group members need to be understood and valued for their success in educational programs. He classified minorities into three subgroups (read Dr. Ogbu's 1978 book, *Minority Education and Caste*):

1.   Voluntary Minorities--This group of minority members assumes minority status based on religion and other cultural values.

However, members of this group operate at the same frequency with members of the dominant society (e.g., the Jews and the Mormons).

2. Immigrant Minorities--This group of minority members is composed of persons who have immigrated from their native countries to the United States to better themselves. Members of this group endure racism and discrimination without mental block about surviving in the dominant society (e.g., Nigerian-Americans, Jamaican-Americans, Japanese-Americans, and Chinese-Americans).

3. Involuntary Minorities--This group of minority members is also called the caste-like minorities. Members of this group have histories of subjugation by the dominant society. Because of incessant dominance, they are skeptical of systems that have resulted from such dominations. Their skepticism is shown through resistance to embodiments of the dominant society (e.g., Native-Americans, Hispanic-Americans, and African-Americans).

Ogbu's theory has several educational implications. First, we have to understand the role of history in the classical conditioning of individuals. Second, minority group members cannot be categorized as one. Third, one-dimensional education produces one-dimensional understanding and thinking . Fourth, there are reasons why some minorities perform better or worse than other minorities. Fifth, history, culture and education cannot be divorced from each other to gain total benefits.

Culture is not a bogeyman. The adage "what you don't know won't hurt you" is counterproductive. In multicultural education, what you know won't hurt you. In other words, "the evil you know is better than the evil that you don't know." I strongly believe we cannot teach what we do not know. We also cannot teach what we have not experienced or experimented on. Education has the uttermost task of connecting individuals with experientialism and experimentalism (see Dr. John Dewey's 1958 classical book, *Philosophy of Education*). Dewey confirmed that:

Education must have a tendency, if it is education, to form attitudes. The tendency to form attitudes which will express themselves in intelligent social action is something very different from indoctrination. . . There is an intermediary between aimless

education and the education of inculcation and indoctrination.
The alternative is the kind of education that connects the
materials and methods by which knowledge is acquired with a
sense of how things are done; not by impregnating the individual
with some final philosophy, whether it comes from Karl Marx or
from Mussolini or Hitler or anybody else, but by enabling him to
so understand existing conditions that an attitude of intelligent
action will follow from social understanding. (p. 56)

Dewey's concept of education has been corroborated today by many
scholars interested in multicultural education. In other words, what is lacking
today is the inability of some educators to understand the correlation between
education and democratic freedom. This lack of understanding has led to the
exclusion of individual members of society in terms of personnel, curriculum
content, and instruction (see Dr. Christine Sleeter's 1992 book, *Keepers of the
American Dream*). My question is, Can we allow this exclusion and/or
miseducation to continue in the 21st century? Teachers and parents have
remarkable roles to play in fostering multicultural education. As Mickler
(1993) pointed out:

Teachers can help all students learn that their intellectual and
academic abilities are far broader than those tested by traditional
assessment techniques and those required to complete the kind of
academic tasks that characterize unidimensional classrooms.
Educators (and parents) must extensively explore their own
personally held views about intelligence and learning and how
those views critically influence their classroom decisions. The
first step is confrontation with a view of intelligence that limits
development of children and contributes to a growing underclass
of students who view themselves as stupid and deficient in the
characteristics valued by their schools and their society. (p. 140)

Most great teachers make an easy transition to multicultural education
because they are capable of incorporating different cultural and instructional
techniques. Most great teachers respect differences within and between
students--they refuse to prejudge their students' capabilities and weaknesses.
As we can see, multicultural education will make teachers good teachers and
good teachers great teachers. It will make teaching fun and put more smiles on
teachers' faces.

In summary, I strongly believe multicultural education has been historically misrepresented. Multicultural teaching does not mean imposing a different language or culture on other Americans. It does not mean Afrocentrism. As an African who is a naturalized citizen of the United States, I think Afrocentrism is similar to Eurocentrism. I believe a balanced education is that which incorporates Afrocentrism, Eurocentrism and Native-American, Hispanic-American, Asian-American and other global cultures into one great curriculum. This combination is not simplistic--it involves collaboration, consultation, inclusion, partnership and cultural diversity. Multicultural teaching challenges teachers to seek new ideas and techniques to reach all students. This can only be successful when we demonstrate willingness to learn and value our styles and differences (see Dr. Barbara Shade's 1989 book, *Culture, Style, and the Educative Process* and Dr. Henry Louis Gates' 1992 book, *Loose Canons: Notes on the Culture Wars*). Logically, when we learn with a smile, there is a strong possibility we will teach with a smile. We model ourselves after our teachers. I concur with the old adage: "We do not stop learning until we are dead." Interestingly, some religions believe in life after death, i.e., that learning never ceases. Simply put, our education must afford us a continuous process of growth. Again, let us not presume, let us learn the facts and let us teach these facts with a smile!

STEP THREE

Change Your Thinking

Let us always remember that those who tyrannize others cannot
ever be free, for they are the slaves of passions, prey to a fixity
of self-interest, which blinds them to the simple truth that
humanity means involvement, involvement in the welfare of
every human-being. And involvement means active engagement
in seeing to it that all children shall be afforded full
opportunities for the realization of their birthright — the
fulfillment of their potential for healthy physical and mental
development. (Montagu, 1986, p. 4)

Montagu (1986) reiterated the 1950 United Nations Educational
Scientific and Cultural Organization "Statement on Race" which indicated that
"national, religious, geographic, linguistic, and cultural groups do not
necessarily coincide with racial groups and the cultural traits of such groups
have not demonstrated genetic connection with racial traits" (p. 4). The issue
of *race* has been a concern amongst member nations. In almost all situations
when I have judged without thinking, I have been wrong. For a long time, I
was biased against a particular religion because someone told me they hated
Blacks. But, my personal experience with people of this religion has shown
they are nice and decent human-beings. Little did I know they have Bishops
from different racial, cultural, linguistic and national backgrounds. Can you
imagine how encouraged I felt when a White lady of that particular religion
wanted to assist me in collecting data for my doctoral dissertation? I was
ashamed of my prejudice!

As I indicated earlier, we all have our biases and prejudices. It is a
human condition to have perceptions about people, events and situations.
Unfortunately, we are unable to acquire knowledge before we judge people,
events and situations. We frequently refuse to search for new meaning (see Dr.
Victor Frankl's 1984 book, *Man's Search for Meaning*). The point is that
ineffective multicultural education and relations are caused by our lack of
knowledge, our prejudice, and our inability to use our "heads." As Gollnich
and Chinn (1990) pointed out, these problems stem from:

A combination of several factors: (1) a lack of understanding of the
history, experiences, values and perceptions of ethnic groups other than

one's own; (2) stereotyping the members of an ethnic group without consideration of individual differences within the group; (3) judging other ethnic groups according to the standards and values of ones's own group; (4) assigning negative attributes to members of other ethnic groups; and (5) evaluating the qualities and experiences of other groups as inferior to one's own. In other words, prejudice and discrimination are extreme forms of ethnocentrism. (p. 89)

Gollnich and Chinn's statement is not limited to one ethnic group. I find it troublesome when some minorities make general statements about White people and vice versa. During the civil rights period, many Whites suffered in their pursuit of freedom for minority group members. Some White people died in Mississippi, and their death has a great educational significance today. We cannot ignore their contributions in history and social studies texts. In South Africa, many Whites lost their lives in the freedom struggle of Africans. It is of historical significance that F. W. de Klerk and Nelson Mandela both won the 1993 Nobel Peace Prize. These individuals have made history. It will be erroneous to ignore either of them in history or social studies books with regard to freedom and liberty because one is Black and the other is White.

I have been told consistently by many African-Americans that I do not look like an African. My response is usually simple: "How does an African look?" I belong to an African-American fraternity (one of my important accomplishments since coming to the United States). Some of my fraternity brothers were skeptical when I wanted to join the fraternity. Thanks to the vision of many distinguished fraternity brothers (e.g., Dr. William McMillan, the President Emeritus of Rust College, Holly Springs, Mississippi), I have another opportunity to touch other lives. In many supposedly progressive African nations ruled by Africans, there have been different forms of prejudices (e.g., tribalism, regionalism, stateism, classism, and religious fanaticism.). Prejudice and discrimination are always enemies to societal progress. Some of my White friends and colleagues tell me I do not act like a Black. Again, my answer is simple: "How do Black people act?" Some even proceed to tell me they do not see my skin color. I appreciate those comments; however, I am bothered that they do not see the best part of me, "my color." My color should be seen as a positive aspect of me. In the United States, color has come to signify negative aspects of many minorities in our educational systems and programs. Using his personal experience as a student of a White teacher, Dr. Shelby Steele (1990b), a conservative African-American scholar, wrote:

The condition of being Black in America means that one will likely endure more wounds to one's self-esteem than others and that the capacity for self-doubt born of these wounds will be compounded and expanded by the Black race's reputation of inferiority... Black skin has more dehumanizing stereotypes associated with it than any other skin color in America, if not the world. When a Black presents himself in an integrated situation, he knows that his skin alone may bring these stereotypes to life in the minds of those he meets and that he, as an individual, may be diminished by his race before he has a chance to reveal a simple aspect of his personality. (p. 36)

Apparently, Steele's Black experience is similar to the experience that many African-Americans or minority group members endure (see Dr. John Hope Franklin's 1980 book, *From Slavery to Freedom*). This experience hinders multicultural education. People's value judgements have to change for multicultural teaching to take place and be successful. We cannot have negative feelings about minority students and expect them to maximize their full potential. Some of these students are already at risk of not succeeding in school. Some come from households mired in poverty, single-parent families and parents or guardians with little education (see Drs. William Davis and Edward McCaul's 1990 Monograph, *At-Risk Children and Youth: A Crisis in Our Schools and Society*). In fact, teachers have to change their mental frameworks to assist minority and/or at-risk students in achieving their goals and objectives. Not long ago, Baer (1991) reiterated:

We need to understand who these kids are. They have potential; however, they don't know it. They need what we all have to offer, but they won't believe it. In a way, they may want to fail because there is a kind of comfort in that. After all, it's what they know best. Failure is a restful place to be. Nobody bothers them much because they can't be expected to give or participate... The crucial point to remember is that in spite of all these obstacles, these kids have all the potential that other kids have. (p. 25)

Baer's comment demonstrates that minority students who are at risk are not well-understood by some professionals who work with them. It implies that nontraditional identification, assessment and instructional strategies are needed to ameliorate their multidimensional problems (McWhirter, McWhirter, McWhirter, & McWhirter, 1993). In addition, it implies that unwarranted suppositions about minorities at all levels do not assist them in becoming productive members of the society (see George Curry's editorial article, "When Being Good Isn't Good Enough," published in the March 1994 issue of *Emerge*).

Changing perceptions about people, events and situations is painstaking. We all have to be willing to leave our comfort zones. When we re-orientate our perceptions, we see observable, measurable and quantifiable variables such as personality changes and how individuals measure or value success through hard-work. Minority students have to positively perceive White teachers, and vice versa. All Whites are not "bad" and all minorities are not "bad." Our thinking has to change and our expectations of people have to change. All minorities are not "lazy" and all Whites are not "racist." Background checks are necessary; judgements without knowledge are unnecessary. No doubt, teachers have to change their perceptions about multicultural education. In the series of workshops and seminars I have conducted, my focus usually has been on the re-orientation of one's thinking before going into the specifics of multicultural teaching. We have to feel that all students are capable; that all cultures can be incorporated into instructional processes. To change belief systems and enhance multicultural teaching, teachers must (a) care for all students, (b) have reasonable expectations of all students, (c) listen to all students, (d) have rewarding environments for all students, and (e) involve all students. These cardinal principles have been followed in my years of teaching.

Currently, I am teaching three courses with 140 White students. Here I am from the Ibo tribe of Nigeria, West Africa teaching all White students in the Midwest of the United States! I continuously believe these students are very capable and I understand and value their cultures. I strongly believe my students are prepared to teach students from different racial, socio-economic, cultural, and linguistic backgrounds. Many of today's public school teachers are not as lucky as my students. They do not have the kind of exposure my students have. The truth is that we cannot allow these good potential teachers to be consumed by the "unknown." We have to really begin to change their thinking.

Legislation meant to heal past wounds for minorities has been somehow ineffective and unproductive. People's perceptions and thinking cannot be legislated. There are many inner-city schools (or schools with students from "poor" homes) that have poor reputations. These schools have been negatively perceived to have "low" quality due to their locations in many communities and due to the kinds of people who attend them. Ironically, year in and year out, these schools graduate top students who have gone to some of the top colleges in this nation. These same schools have White teachers (and only a few minority teachers) who make their living teaching minority students. There is also a negative perception that parents of these students do not care about their children's education and future. With all these negative perceptions, how can multicultural teaching be encouraged and enhanced? Again, the fact remains that many inner-city schools are poorly funded (read Jonathan Kozol's 1991 book, *Savage Inequalities*). Why can't the American press highlight the tremendous works done by great teachers and students in these inner-city schools? Sometimes I wonder if we are really concerned about problems confronting minority students or the politics of these problems.

I have never been a great fan of Affirmative Action regulations because of their misuse in the betrayal of human dignity. I have had many humorous experiences from being the "first" or the "only" Black person. As a student, I was the "only" and "first" Black student in my college classes. Some of my classmates were well-prepared and others were not. I was always being patronized or paternalized. When I refused to be patronized or paternalized, some of them felt I was arrogant and out of character. It was apparent that I was the most underrated, yet I excelled more than most of my classmates (see Dr. Shelby Steele's 1990a book, *The Content of Our Character)*. On one occasion, I told one of my professors that I did a library search on Nigeria's educational system, but was unable to find pertinent materials. The professor laughed and said: "Who needs them anyway?" He thought it was funny; however, it depicts how much multicultural education is needed at all echelons of American education. At a point, I wanted him to sign an important document for me and he indicated: "You remind me of my teenage daughter who wants and wants." This professor forgot that I wanted the kind of support he gave to his other White students. Not long ago, I was in a conversation with this same professor and he expressed surprise about my success since graduating from college. He said: "You have excelled more than our other graduates. What has happened to our graduates?" I briefly responded: "Nothing has happened to your graduates; maybe you overrated them and underrated me. That is why you are surprised." He was silent for a moment and stated: "You are right." Underrating minorities in our educational programs occurs from pre-kindergarten to post-doctoral levels. Pretending that such an action does not exist is counterproductive to multicultural learning and teaching. For further reading, see Dr. Cornel West's 1993 book, *Race Matters*.

When I started interviewing for jobs, some colleges were interested in how "nice" I was or how much I "fit into" their programs and not how "capable" I was. I rejected many jobs because of this; and many rejected me because I was not nice enough. Minority individuals have been continuously forced to fit into systems and programs. Would it not be refreshing to see programs fit into minority individuals' needs for a change? This is the essence of multicultural teaching, i.e., to make classroom programs fit into the needs of minority students. I still wonder why my White colleagues were judged on their "capabilities" and why I was judged on "likeness" or "niceness." Likeness, as we know it, is not a measurable variable--it is frequently based on perception. In one university, a White female colleague reminded me that my position was a desegregation position. In other words, she wanted me to mind my P's and Q's. Fascinating! I had always thought that women are treated as minorities in the workplace. In this same university, I won the "Researcher of the Year" award two years in a row. In another university, the Dean came to my office twice a week with the statement: "Let me know how I can help you." It got so bad that my heart pounded each time I saw him. He was extremely paternalistic and patronizing. I am sure he thought he was doing the right thing. Would it not have been collegial if he invited me for lunch those many times as he invited my other White colleagues?

These experiences have been rewarding. I have learned from all of them. No doubt, we all can learn from them. We are reminded of how much we are in dire need of multicultural learning and teaching at all levels. Many minorities, like their White peers, believe in hard-work and productivity. We need to give them the opportunity, and we need to think of them as capable human-beings. To survive in the 21st century, our thinking has to change to respond to the needs of all students, irrespective of their racial, cultural and linguistic backgrounds. We can never assume all Whites are one way and all minorities are the other way. We can only clear our doubts by re-orientating our thinking. When we do this, we have accomplished 50% of multicultural learning and teaching. Only then can we know that multicultural education is fun.

Many teachers are afraid of change. This fear gives them one more reason not to smile. They perceive change to be a dangerous phenomenon. In reality, we have to acknowledge change or we will be consumed by change. Put another way, change is a reality whose time has come. We must change our thinking about students--our students are getting more sophisticated than we credit them. For instance, one of my students (a White male) in the Survey of Exceptionality course, Mr. Lee Owens on March 11, 1994 sent me a brief note. He wanted me to share his note with his classmates. He wrote:

Dear Dr. Obiakor:

We had the assistant principal come talk to the class [the Phase I
class] about observation in the high school. He said it was ok to
get involved in tutoring a student who has trouble but he was not
going to put us with a special education student who "can't
learn." That was what he told the class. Instead of having
"new" teachers take your class, you (Dr. Obiakor) need to have
"old" teachers and administrators take your class.

Lee Owens.

From Mr. Owen's note, we could sense some frustration. There are
many young enthusiastic individuals like Mr. Owens out there -- these
individuals find themselves between "the deep sea and the devil" as they
attempt to shift their paradigms. These individuals understand that their
demographics are changing, and they want to change; but the "power brokers"
refuse to change. Evidently, if we think retrogressively, we cannot engage in
multicultural learning and teaching. In Summer 1993, I was invited by the
Region VII School District, Kilgore, Texas, to conduct a series of workshops
for teachers and administrators. These workshops were well-organized and I
saw teachers and administrators with great enthusiasm. However, I sensed
inside this enthusiasm was fear on how to handle our changing demographics.
My message to my audience was that we must be willing to deal with change.
The first step must start with how we think about people, events and situations
(see Acel Moore's article, "Need Someone to Blame? Just Say a Black Man
Did It" published in the March 25, 1994 issue of *The Wichita Eagle*).
Politicians can appeal to people by scaring them, but teachers cannot afford to
run away from their responsibilities.

Our world is not static. Who would have thought that the Soviet Union
would change? Who would have thought that an Israeli leader would have
shaken hands with a Palestinian Liberation Organization (PLO) leader? Our
ideas about change as a construct have to change if we are going to respond
effectively to multicultural teaching. In his book, *The Third Wave*, Alvin
Toffler (1982) challenged us all when he wrote:

The responsibility for change, therefore, lies with us. We must begin
with ourselves, teaching ourselves not to close our minds prematurely to
the novel, the surprising, the seemingly radical. This means fighting off

idea assassins who rush forward to kill any new suggestion on grounds of its impracticality, while defending whatever now exists as practical, no matter how absurd, oppressive, or unworkable it may be. It means fighting for freedom of expression, the right to voice their ideas even if heretical. (p. 443)

In summary, Toffler's statement challenges teachers and other professionals involved in the educational process to respond to change. We cannot continue to pretend by using simplistic assumptions which are deficit-oriented. Many years ago, Weikert (1977) warned that the deficit model, when applied to a certain population, "seems to limit potential assistance to that group because it channels thinking in ways that emphasize weaknesses rather than strengths, and it interprets differences from the norm as individual deficits" (p. 75). Let's change our thinking! Let's not give up! Let's be proud of our accomplishments as teachers! When we believe in ourselves, there is all likelihood that we will believe in all our students. We have to think we can because if we think we can't we will never be able to handle the challenges and joys of multicultural learning and teaching.

STEP FOUR

Use Resource Persons

You declare you see me dimly
through a glass which will not shine,
though I stand before you boldly,
trim in rank and marking time.

You do own to hear me faintly
as a whisper out of range
while my drums beat out the message
and the rhythms never change.

Equality, and I will be free
Equality, and I will be free.

(These three stanzas are from "Equality," one of the poems in Maya Angelou's 1990 book, *I Shall Not be Moved*.)

As most teachers, I do not like my territory to be invaded. I have been educated (not trained or indoctrinated) to do my job. Most teachers feel the same way. Majority of teachers love their job. There are a few who do not quite know the impact of their job on young minds. Just as multiculturalism has become a buzzing concept, collaboration, consultation, inclusion and partnership have also become buzzwords. We are seriously preparing for the 21st century. We know our demographics are changing. This book began with a recounting of my visit with elementary students. Can you imagine the miseducation that had taken place before my presentation? Can you imagine how relieved the students were? Can you imagine why I found it difficult to discredit the students' teacher? The truth of the matter is that she invited me to speak to her students because she wanted me to give first-hand information and probably authenticate what she had taught them. I do not know if I authenticated her teaching; however, I gave first-hand information to her students. I respect teachers like her.

Resource persons are very useful. In Denise Magner's (1993) article, "When Whites teach Black Studies" published in the December issue of *The Chronicle of Higher Education*, African-American students in many predominantly White colleges are resenting the fact that White professors are teaching African-American history in Black Studies departments. These students have argued that Afrocentric perspectives seem to be void in many classes. Even experienced White teachers in the field have suffered the wrath of these students (see Dr. Christie Farnham Pope's article, "The Challenge Posed by Radical Afrocentrism When a White Professor Teaches Black History" published in the March 30, 1994 issue of *The Chronicle of Higher Education*). In my opinion, there is nothing wrong with knowledgeable Whites teaching Black Studies courses. But, something is wrong when they fail to present all perspectives or collaborate with resource persons when necessary. White teachers must continue to teach in Black Studies departments as long as they use resource persons in difficult-to-explain topics or when they feel their biases might intrude in their instructions. It is erroneous to think skin color is positively correlated with Black Studies knowledge. This is why multicultural teaching is needed at all levels of education. I was once a guest in a Black History course; and discussions arose about the role of Carribeans in African-American politics, culture and education. A notable name during this discussion was Marcus Garvey of Jamaica who immigrated to the United States and was deeply involved in African-American issues. One African-American student in this class asked an interesting question: "What part of Africa is Jamaica?" I was amazed that this student, a senior majoring in history, was unaware of the location of Jamaica, West Indies. It is dangerous to assume all Blacks are knowledgeable about Black history or all Hispanics are well-versed in Hispanic history.

Colleges and universities have roles to play in providing and producing resource persons for communities in which they exist. According to Dr. Ernest Boyer (1994), the President of the Carnagie Foundation for the Advancement of Teaching, "higher education and the larger purposes of American society have been — from the very first — inextricably intertwined" (p. A48). He added:

> I'm concerned that in recent years, higher education's historic
> commitment to service seems to have diminished. I'm troubled
> that many now view the campus as a place where professors get
> tenured and students get credentialed; the overall efforts of the
> academy are not considered to be at the vital center of the
> nation's work. And what I find most disturbing is the growing
> feeling in this country that higher education is a *private* benefit,
> *not* a public good. . . . .
> . . . Some students are successful, but far too many are

educationally deficient, often dropping out. What we're facing
in education is not just academic failure, but also drugs,
violence, and alienation—problems that cannot be solved by
simply adding more requirements for graduation. Do colleges
really believe they can ignore the social pathologies that
surround schools and erode the educational foundations of our
nation? (p. A48)

It is evident from Dr. Boyer's statement that colleges and universities must
provide programs and resources that link them to their communities. In many
predominantly White colleges and universities, the roles of directors of
minority programs have not been very well-defined. They are looked upon as
Affirmative Action exclusionary programs rather than appreciated for the real
roles that they play. In her essay, "My Experiences as Director of a
Multicultural Center," Dr. Carolyn Princes (1994) identified her duties as the
Director of the Black Cultural Center at Indiana University of Pennsylvania.
She explained:

My office's primary role is the enhancement of multicultural
awareness and racial sensitivity dynamics for the university and
community. Practically, I focus on cultural programming, i.e.,
the provision of activities that are of particular interest to
African-American students and the university community. The
Black Cultural Center serves as a place for formal and informal
exchanges for university faculty, staff, administrators, and
students. The encompassing goal is to demonstrate cultural
differences while promoting an appreciation for those
differences. My experiences have been professionally rewarding
and enriching and at times, frustrating, disappointing, and
stressful. Basically, I have found that a multicultural office is
unlike any other office on a university campus.
Administratively, one gets to wear all hats. Sometimes,
loneliness overrides. Being a Director has helped to diffuse the
myth that only African-American students have needs and the
dangerous myth that minorities cannot successfully complete a
college curriculum. My message is that college needs are cross-
cultural and intercultural. In fact, I find myself as an advocate,
teacher, administrator, counselor, advisor, driver, medical
assistant, liaison, etc. My greatest reward occurs when I see

these supposedly "high-risk" students graduate from college. In summary, the benefits of a Director's efforts may not be immediately known, however, they often far exceed the problems he/she might face. The importance of my office cannot be underestimated. We teach and learn; and we advocate for and provide resources to the campus community. Very often, we get to be utilized as resource persons for public schools and the general community. (p. 1)

How will we know who knows what unless we learn and teach? To avoid any miseducation, we must learn the facts and use resource persons when in doubt. As teachers, we cannot continue to give inaccurate information to our students. As the old adage goes: "We can deceive some of the people all the time, but we cannot deceive all the people all the time." Many of the books on African history in American schools have been written by White scholars. Some of these books have presented complete and accurate information, and others have presented incomplete and inaccurate information that does not help in multicultural learning and teaching. For example, there have been debates on the color of Cleopatra, an ancient African queen. How many people know that Egypt, Morocco and Libya are in Africa? Apparently, many important aspects of history are lost when misinformation takes precedence over truth. For further information, read Dr. Talmadge Anderson's 1993 book, *Introduction to African-American Studies*. When discussions are focused on the Egyptian Pyramids, the intelligence of Africans is rarely highlighted. Who is to blame? Many Egyptian leaders play two roles. On the one hand, they are strong participants in the Organization of African Unity (OAU) where cultural and political policies are made regarding independent African nations. On the other hand, they are strong participants in the Middle East politics because of historical, religious and cultural ties. These explanations need to be made in history, geography and social studies classes in American schools at elementary, high-school and college levels. For instance, I was particularly pleased when I was invited on March 16, 1994, by a veteran teacher (Mrs. Judy Schwenn) to her Emporia High School 10th grade English class. My assignment was to read poetry and explicate my experiences from Nigeria to the United States. These students were very interested in my stories because they could relate to them inspite of our cultural differences. The only Black in this class was myself, the presenter. However, my stories made them think -- it was evident when one of the students volunteered to read one of my poems, "To Be A Man" in the book, *The Twisted Faith* (Obiakor,

1992a) which reads:

> To be a man
> is to care for your family.
>
> To be a man
> is to produce for your society.
>
> To be a man
> is to respect your values.
>
> To be a man
> is to protect your dignity.
>
> To be a man
> is to educate mankind.
>
> To be a man
> is to uplift humanity.

Apparently, there are educational implications of my service to these students. First, multicultural learning and teaching took place. Second, these White students now know that inspite of cultural differences, people can have similar values. Third, these students have now seen an educated Black man -- this will go a long way to reduce their negative perceptions, if any. Fourth, these students are exposed to somebody from a university environment. Fifth, we now see an excellent example of partnership and collaboration between university and community. This latter implication was obvious when I not only received a letter of thanks from the students and teacher, but also from a parent. See below the parent's March 18, 1994 letter to me:

Dear Dr. Obiakor:

I want to thank you for sharing your poetry, life, etc. with my son's high school English class this past week. He came home so enthused - he was sure you and he were now on a first name basis! He took two of your poems to share with a church group on their way to the United Nations today to study ethnic cleansing. Thanks for sharing your time and talents.

Mrs. Paula Sauder.

As we have seen, the university has an important role to play in reducing some of the societal problems. This role can be played in many different ways. We must encourage Whites to be involved in scholarly works related to African-American history and education. In The Teachers College of my university, people leading discussions on minority issues are White males and females. Should we dissuade them from their interests because they are Whites? In fact, the more Whites who are involved in discourse on minority issues the better. How retrogressive will it be for Whites to dissuade minorities from studying and writing about European history? It might be unproductive to cry "wolf" when it is unnecessary. The more resource persons we produce the better, race and culture notwithstanding. How can multicultural learning and teaching be enhanced if we do not involve everyone in the process?

A wise man once stated: "Do not believe all you read!" Some books give students skewed information. For instance, there have been tremendous debates on the founding of America by Christopher Columbus. We cannot totally discredit history, but we can add a lot to history. In such a class discussion, inviting Native-Americans would be a good idea. Sure, we have to give credit to the gallantry of Christopher Columbus and his entourage. However, we have to give credit to those Native-Americans who were living here before he came. For further information, read Dr. Joel Spring's 1994 book, *Deculturalization and the Struggle for Equality.* There are distinguished minority members of every community; and their perspectives can be considered in school reforms and curricula changes. When we ignore them, we have actually "scratched the snake, but not killed it." My father once told me that "a problem unsolved is still a problem no matter how you look at it." I still remember being invited to read poetry (Négritude poetry) to employees of the Tennessee Valley Authority during Black History Month celebrations. I have honored similar invitations in pre-school, elementary, middle school, high school and college programs to speak to students. The business communities and educational foundations cannot downplay the impact of minority participation in the community. After all, most businesses do not locate or relocate in communities that do not take education of all students seriously. It is no wonder that the business community plays a great role in recruiting and hiring university presidents, superintendents, and even school principals.

Let's go back to our classrooms! In educating individuals who are exceptional, the law requires that team work prevails during identification, assessment, placement and instruction. Regular teachers should feel secure involving special educators, speech and language pathologists, physical therapists, medical doctors, psychologists, parents and students when necessary. Resource persons are needed at all aspects of education. Again, "two heads are better than one." In the book that he edited with Dr. Thomas Lovitt, *Integrating General and Special Education*, Dr. John Goodlad (1993) emphasized:

> The greater integration of special and general education is an educational development long overdue. Effecting it stirs and rearranges an extraordinary political, economic, and educational network of agencies, institutions, and individuals... Significant change affects entire ecosystems, arousing passions, changing human behaviors, and exposing reefs not marked on any charts... Because significant change is torturous and wearing for those involved and affected, major actions frequently become both tired and myopic and ultimately settle for something falling far short of what is necessary. This has been to a considerable degree the case in desegregating schools and mainstreaming. (p. 31)

The collaboration between teachers and other professionals has several implications. The notable significance is that professionals can work together with mutual respect for each other (Boyles, 1990). Students can then model themselves after these professionals. They will begin to respect each other--this kind of respect has some far-reaching effects on conflict resolution and multicultural education. My hunch is that we cannot continue to talk about multicultural teaching without mutual respect for different professionals who provide services for all students. As professionals, we have to be ethical to teach ethics and morality. Hypocrisy is an enemy of multicultural learning and teaching. It creates mistrust and hinders communication. Trust and communication are major thrusts of multicultural education (read Dr. Adelbert Jenkins' 1982 book, *The Psychology of the Afro-American: A Humanistic Approach* and Dr. David Matsumoto's 1994 book, *People: Psychology from a Cultural Perspective*). Trust and communication facilitate understanding of the following processes:

1.   The nature of human perception and thinking.

2.   Language characteristics of different people.

3.   Multiple channels of seeing, hearing, and touching.

4.   The state of mind of individuals involved.

5.   Mixed messages of people.

6.   Complete and incomplete interactions of people.

7.   Conscious and unconscious verbal signals of individuals.

8.   Conscious and unconscious nonverbal signals of individuals.

9.   The climate and purpose of interpersonal interactions of different people.

10.   Intentional/unintentional information from and to people.

The partnership between teachers and parents is compulsory for multicultural learning and teaching to occur and proceed. It is wrong for teachers to assume that parents of minority students are incapable because of their socio-economic or socio-political status (see Dr. Beth Harry's 1992 book, *Cultural Diversity, Families, and the Special Education System: Communication and Empowerment* and Dr. Sonia Nieto's 1992 book, *Affirming Diversity*). Today, education is dominated by the myth of socio-economic dissonance. "Poverty" has no bearing on intelligence, self-concept and zest to succeed in life. It is equally wrong for parents of minority students to think that all White teachers hate them and their children. Parents cannot continue to use "poverty" as an alibi for irresponsible parenting. This wall of mistrust has to be broken down to allow for healthy communication. The rationale for empowering parents of White students should be the rationale for empowering parents of minority students.

Parents of minority students can be excellent resource persons to school systems and classroom instructions, especially when multicultural issues are involved. I have three young children. They have consistently been the only African-Americans in their classes. Their teachers have been surprised that we have been as caring as we are. They have been also fascinated to see that I (a

Black male) have devoted my time to the excellent education of my children. Not long ago, I went to pick up my children and they ran to me with excitement shouting, "Daddy, Daddy, Daddy." One of their teachers yelled, "Stop running! Don't be so excited." As a parent whose children are the only African-Americans in the school, I did not want to upset this teacher. I wanted to see if this teacher would repeat this disciplinary approach. Lo and behold, I went some other time to pick up my children. Again, my children showed some excitement shouting, "Daddy, Daddy, Daddy" and as usual ran to me. The same teacher yelled, "Don't run! Why all the excitement?" Again, I did not want to offend this teacher. I called the director of the day care and wanted to know the rationale for such a disciplinary approach. Her response was that they had always done that and there was no rationale. I responded: "If it ain't broke, don't fix it! I want to see my children happy and excited all the time, especially when I come to pick them up." Being an excellent director, she knew that was a Eurocentric disciplinary method that had no basis for my African-American children. I did not want my children to be labeled very early as having behavior problems just because they got excited when they saw their parents. As in my case, parents of minority students could be consulted and utilized in conflict resolution in school and classroom programs. But, if we already have a mental block toward them, how can we involve and use them as resource persons in times of need? It is a "win, win" situation when parents of minority students are used as resource persons. In that case, teachers do not have to go very far to research cultures, beliefs, languages and histories of their minority students. To effectively increase parental empowerment and partnership, teachers should:

1. Hold meetings at convenient places.

2. Encourage parent input.

3. Desist from making unwarranted suppositions about parents.

4. Follow-up after meetings with parents.

5. Have realistic expectations of parents.

It should be noted that many parents of minority students are knowledgeable. They should be given the opportunity to share this knowledge, especially when multicultural education is taking place in classes. By getting involved, they can reduce instructional costs, compensate for manpower shortages and solve problems of time and distance. As teachers continue to use resource persons and build safety nets for all persons, all their students will begin to reap the benefits of multicultural learning and teaching.

As we have seen, anyone can be a valuable resource person. All resource persons are not knowledgeable about multicultural learning and teaching. On the one hand, that someone is an African-American, an Hispanic or a Native-American does not make that individual the sole authority on minority issues. On the other hand, a very knowledgeable minority will serve many purposes. He or she will help to reduce negative perceptions about minorities with a mere presence. Let us look at the following cases:

Case #1

An African-American superintendent of a school district was hired to respond to multicultural issues confronting the schools. For some reason, he had the habit of not inviting African-American specialists on multicultural issues. He consistently invited White women and ignored African-American resource persons to appeal to the powers-that-be in that city.

Case #2

A school district was under pressure to address multicultural issues. The superintendent (a White male) had the habit of inviting very conservative African-American males. By doing this, he alienated the minority constituency. There was a tremendous outcry for his removal.

Case #3

A county school district prides itself on quality and excellence in education. The superintendent (a White male) does not believe in full inclusion of minority and exceptional students in school programs. In fact, this district does not respond to federal laws meant to address this issue. To achieve this aim of "quality without equity," the superintendent hired three attorneys who are bent on maintaining this phony standard.

Case #4

A particular university that I was affiliated with spent so much money inviting minority speakers who were extremely liberal. This university got the publicity, and gave the impression that it was for multicultural issues. However, it had three minority faculty members, and none was tenured. There was a pattern of not continuing minority faculty members after some years of service, and recruiting new ones. There were always minority faculty members but no commitment to tenure them. There was also no commitment to make the university environment conducive to minority faculty and students. This university had the "revolving door" mentality, yet it brought in some "top guns" to speak on campus. By error or design, this institution was playing the self-destructive Affirmative Action game.

The four cases are only but a few of how institutions have tried to use resource persons incorrectly. Multicultural teaching is not an Affirmative Action gimmick. It is a demonstrable commitment to involve all persons (Whites and minorities) to educate all students. In Case #1, there was nothing wrong with inviting knowledgeable White women. The superintendent, however, had to be careful of not alienating minorities in an attempt to please the powers-that-be. In Case #2, conservative African-American males must never be excluded in the discussions. They have good messages that could help alleviate problems confronting African-American communities. However, we have to be careful that we do not alienate other communities. Case #3 basically explains the "old" ways of conflict resolution. Does it not make sense to use the money paid to attorneys to provide equitable education for all students? Communities have to play dominant roles in involving all persons in educating all students. Case #4 depicts how many predominately White colleges play the Affirmative Action game instead of using all persons to educate all students. This game must not be allowed to continue if we are to deal realistically with multicultural learning and teaching in schools and communities. Again, let us use all persons (Whites and minorities) to educate all students at all levels!

In summary, our ability to correctly use resource persons will demonstrate our willingness to leave our comfort zones and search for new meanings. It is important that we recognize the difficulty in this worthy search. As the late Dr. Martin Luther King, Jr. pointed out:

Human progress is neither automatic nor inevitable. Even a superficial look at history reveals that no social advance rolls in on the wheels of inevitability. Every step toward the goal of justice requires sacrifice, suffering, and struggle, the tireless exertions and passionate concern of dedicated individuals.

Without persistent effort, time itself becomes an ally of the insurgent and primitive forces of irrational emotionalism and social destruction. This is no time for apathy or complacency. This is a time for vigorous and positive action. (King, 1983, p. 59)

STEP FIVE

Build Self-Concepts

While all students deserve to have their islands of competence
displayed and built upon, there is a more urgent need to do so
for those students who lack confidence in their ability to learn. If
we can find and reinforce the areas of strength these students
possess, my experience has been that we can open the way for a
"ripple effect," where students may be willing to venture forth
and confront tasks that have been problematic for them.
(Brooks, 1991, p. 32)

Many of our young children are robbed of their self-esteem and the
capacity to achieve. Being a minority broadens the multidimensional scope of
problems confronting our youth. In many instances due to cultural differences,
minority students are at risk of having "low" self-concepts. The exceptions are
students whose parents develop a "positive" self-concept early. These are
children who arrive at school with the desire to achieve and be productive, the
ability to accept personal success as well as failure, and skillfulness in setting
and reaching realistic goals (Behrmann, 1991).

When there is no push by families to build a "positive" self-concept,
many minority children come to school lacking confidence and hope for their
future. In such cases, these students do not adjust to the learning environment,
lack the desire to try, and aspire to unrealistic goals. What follows in their
schooling are self-defeating behaviors. Logically, when these students try but
fail at a task, they are likely to place blame externally, attributing low grades to
a teacher's prejudice against their skin color or factors unrelated to their
performance. Also a problem is some teachers, who out of caring, fail to
challenge minority students enough and thereby reinforce mediocre efforts.
When this happens, these students become known as "lazy," "not serious," or
as students "trying to get by" with minimal effort. These misimpressions
become labels on minority students--they negatively affect their self-concepts
as they fail to live up to their potential.

I have mentioned the construct "self-concept" several times. What is
self-concept? How important is self-concept to multicultural learning and
teaching? Self-concept is an important educational phenomenon which
traditionally cuts across identification, assessment and instructional programs
for minority students. This importance notwithstanding, divergent viewpoints

have been generated to make assessment and pedagogy very intriguing. In working with minority students, the contemporary or operational viewpoint which sees self-concept as an individual's repertoire of self-descriptive behavior has proven to be more effective and productive, especially in designing Individualized Education Programs (IEPs). Self-concept has continued to be the primary focus of programs for minority and disadvantaged students, yet it continues to mean different things to different people. The variability in the definition, assessment and interpretation of self-concept has, to a large extent, led to the proliferation of measurement tools. Time and time again, we have heard the following statement:

> By the time a child reaches school age his self-concept is well formed and his reactions to learning, to school failure and success and to physical, social and emotional climate of the classroom will be determined by the beliefs and attitudes he has about himself. (Canfield & Wells, 1976, p. 3)

The above supposition indicates that a change in self-concept is likely to affect a wide range of behaviors. When one aspect of the child's self-concept is affected, there is a "domino effect" on his/her entire self-concept. Applying this model of self-concept in the classroom will require the involvement with the minority student's school and home life. Such a practice will place the teacher in a rather precarious position of encouraging classroom discussion on aspects of the child's life which are outside the primary domain of the school's delegated responsibility. Moreover, this practice encourages student labeling or categorization and hampers classroom learning and/or functional learning outcomes. It becomes educationally unproductive to use this conceptualization of self-concept in regular, special or inclusive classrooms, especially in designing IEPs for minority students (Obiakor, 1992b).

It is important to note that traditional instruments used to measure self-concept have produced consistent results but have failed to measure what they purport to measure. How can an instrument measure the construct that it does not define? How can the strengths and weaknesses of minority students be identified when the interpretation of results is globally based on the "positive" or "negative" and "high" or "low" perspectives? Evidently, teachers should interpret self-concept of minority students with caution. Very often, traditional tests measure what is positive according to the social ideal of the dominant society (Obiakor, Stile & Muller, 1993). Since teachers know the importance of self-concept, they should think about self-concept of minority students in terms that can be described, observed and explained. Put another way, self-concept should be viewed by teachers as a self-descriptive behavior; and like all self-descriptive behaviors, it can be measured. I prefer to break down self-concept into three major areas (read Obiakor and Stile's 1993 book, *Self-Concept of Exceptional Learners: Current Perspectives for Educators*):

1. Self-knowledge: This tells who the student is by his or her characteristics or qualities.

2. Self-esteem: This reveals a student's likes and dislikes of personal characteristics according to how a child values them.

3. Self-ideal: This exposes qualities the student wants to achieve personally through self-empowerment.

Each of these can be assessed in terms of physical maturity, peer relations, academic success, and school adaptiveness. Before trying to build self-concept through teaching, teachers must first understand its changing nature, and its potential to be accurate or inaccurate, covert or overt, and different from one situation to the next. Self-concept measurement, then, should take place in a context similar to that in which the results will be used. Because self-concept is not predetermined, teachers can use instruction to enhance it. The techniques that work best involve direct teaching, modifying the environment, employing intrinsic motivation, and helping to put failure into perspective. It is very easy to build or destroy self-concepts of all students. The cases below exemplify the predicaments of minority students in today's public schools (read Dr. Carter G. Woodson's 1933 classical book, *The Mis-Education of the Negro*):

Case #5

I visited an inner-city elementary school to see my student-teacher. I was fortunate to meet the principal of the school (a White female) who started telling me that all her students came from "poor" homes, and that they never did well in school because their parents did not have jobs. During our conversation, she told me that she lived in the suburb and that she drove sixty miles every day to and from school.

Case #6

I visited an inner-city high school to observe my student-teacher. In my conversation with the cooperating teacher (a White male), he told me that his students were "poor" and that many of them were drug-dealers who would either not succeed in life or would die before they became adults. When I asked him about solutions to help them, he laughed and indicated that it was difficult to "flog a dead horse."

Case #7

I visited my student-teacher in a resource room in one of the inner-city elementary schools. The cooperating teacher was an African-American female with an Educational Specialist (Ed.S) degree in Special Education. During my conversation with her, she proceeded to tell me that many of her students were criminals. She particularly pointed out one of her students -- she told me that the student had broken into cars several times and that the student's mother was a prostitute. When I asked why she was telling me this awful story she noted that everybody knew.

Case #8

I visited an inner-city elementary school to continue my program, Project Self-Responsibility, which I initiated to help retain and graduate African-American students. The principal (an African-American male) was very nonchalant. He explained that the reasons for his skepticism were (a) these students were jail-birds who came from "poor" homes, and (b) these students' parents did not have jobs. In our conversation, he indicated that these students were beyond redemption.

The problems of minority and/or at-risk students identified above might seem unthinkable; however, they do not end at elementary and high school levels. Consider the cases below:

Case #9

An Hispanic-American male is a college freshman who was good in both history and the sciences. He was advised by his high school counselor to major in history and not the sciences. When he took the interest inventory in college, he found that he was more interested in the sciences. He is now majoring in "pre-med" with a grade point of 3.8 out of 4.0.

Case #10

An African-American male is a wide-receiver for his university's football team. He is now a senior who plans to attend law school. For four years, even though he is one of the top students in his classes, his White peers and professors have made implicit racist remarks about African-Americans and sports.

Case #11

In a history class, a White male professor exalted the achievements of White Americans in building America. The only Native-American in the class asked, "Don't you think minorities have helped in building America?" The professor ignored him. A White student remarked very rudely, "Why can't these minorities go back to where they came from?" Everyone (including the professor) laughed. Again, the professor continued his discussions without responding to the issues.

Case #12

An African-American male was the only minority in his department and College/School. He was treated with disrespect by his White peers and regarded as a desegregation (Affirmative Action) quota by his peers and students. He complained several times, but no one listened. Even though, he was productive, he was discontinued or let go by his university because "he could not get along with others." He is now seeking a legal redress.

The above cases (Cases 5-12) demonstrate how tradition conflicts with reality. What one individual may call tradition may constitute real problems for another individual. When a group of people is viewed as "poor" and/or "deprived," it shows an inability to confront real problems of real people. We cannot assume that members of minority groups cannot learn and at the same time expect them to perform academic, social and economic miracles. In her chapter, "The Self and the Black Male: Implications for School and Society," Dr. Narviar Cathcart Barker (1993) decried the continuous denigration of Blacks in the society. She wrote:

> The peculiarity exists that youth internalize or define others' actions toward them as factual information and interpretations about themselves rather than as social interactions or as explications that may not be valid. Their acceptance of this

information is based upon the perceived influence and status of
the individual rendering such information. Therefore when the
Black child's environment labels him as expendable or
superfluous, and then responds to him as such, the internalization
of these messages has long lasting and severe consequences.
(p. 172)

These cases demonstrate attempts (by error or design) to deflate self-concepts
of individuals. The dangerous response has been for minority group members
to internalize these negative actions rather than demonstrate through
performance and outcomes that they are capable. The result is that everyone
blames everyone without self-responsibility. We all lose when this happens. I
am reminded of inscriptions in the June 1993 cartoon published by Joel Pett in
Pett Peeves which read as follows:

SEE DICK!

DICK IS POOR!

SEE DICK'S GRADES.
ALSO POOR!

SEE DICK'S FAMILY
BLAME THE SCHOOL!

SEE THE SCHOOL
BLAME DICK'S FAMILY!

SEE DICK'S FUTURE?
NEITHER CAN DICK.

Teachers are sometimes unaware of the positive or negative impact
of their perceptions and expectations. In most school programs, students liked
by their teachers are frequently assumed to have accurate or "positive"
self-concepts, and when they are not liked, they are assumed to have "low"
self-concepts. In one of my classes, my student brought a fable to share with
me and the rest of her classmates. This fable has an Unknown Author, but it
exemplifies how teachers' expectations can affect self-concepts and
achievements in classes. Below is the fable:

Once upon a time the animals had a school. The curriculum consisted of running, climbing, flying, and swimming, and all the animals took *all* the subjects. The duck was good in swimming; better, in fact, than his instructor. He made passing grades in flying, but he was particularly hopeless in running. Because he was low in this subject, he was made to stay in after school and drop his swimming class in order to practice running. He kept this up until he was only average in swimming. But average was acceptable, so nobody worried about that - except the duck. The eagle was considered a problem pupil and was severely disciplined because, although he beat all the others to the top of the tree in the climbing class, he insisted on using his own method. The rabbit started out at the top of the class in running, but he had a nervous breakdown and had to drop out of school because of so much makeup work in swimming. The squirrel led the class in climbing, but his flying teacher made him start his flying lessons from the ground up instead of from the top of the tree down. He developed charley horses from overexertion at the takeoff and began getting Cs in climbing and Ds in running. The practical prairie dogs apprenticed their offspring to the badger when the school authorities refused to add digging to the curriculum. At the end of the year, an abnormal eel that could swim well, run a few feet, climb a bit, and fly a little was made valedictorian.

The above fable tells us that teachers play a great role in uplifting or downgrading their students. Sometimes, teachers and administrators give confusing signals. For example, in her essay titled, "The Plight of Black Students in Public Schools," Mrs. Chiquita Ballenger (1994) described how self-concepts of African-American students have been strategically destroyed by some public schools. In her opinion, this destruction is due to the lack of role models and inadequate curriculum in public schools (see Dr. Molefi Asante's 1987 book, *The Afrocentric Idea*). As Mrs. Ballenger recounted:

Being a veteran educator in the Texas public school system for 15 years has revealed many ways Black children are exploited academically and emotionally. By so doing, their self-concepts are destroyed. My first concern is the hiring and/or retention of Black educators, and my second concern is curriculum relevancy and design. In order for public schools to be effective in building self-concepts of Black children, there must be a balance between minority and White faculty. For example, in one school where I taught, there were approximately 45 teachers. Of the 45, six where Black and only one was a male. This imbalance between minority and White teachers begins from kindergarten and extends to the 12th grade. Where then are the role models for growing Black children? How then can these students' self-concepts be enhanced under the circumstances? The second concern is even more important than the first concern. How can Black students feel good about themselves when they cannot see themselves in the curriculum? Most lessons leave Black students with slim opportunities to apply acquired skills and knowledge. It has been my experience that much of the teaching in some public schools generate frustration and low self-esteem for many Black children. How beneficial is it to repeatedly tell Black children about Christopher Columbus' discovery of America and never teach them about Crispus Attucks, Benjamin Banneker and Frederick Douglas? Curricula designs and lessons avoid reinforcing the positive aspects of Black American culture. All these concerns when combined force Black children to lose their self-identities. (p. 1)

The concerns highlighted by Mrs. Ballenger are similar to concerns of many minority scholars and educators. Personally, I do not believe there is a conspiracy to destroy minority students. As I indicated earlier, there are many factors that affect the accuracy or inaccuracy of self-concepts of these students. Efforts must be made by Whites and minorities to reduce perceptions or situations that perpetuate negative labels. When public schools perceive minorities as incapable, they fail to accurately interpret their self-concepts and academic capabilities. In the same direction, when members of minority groups ineffectively perceive public schools, they do some disservice to themselves in their interpretation of students' self-concepts and academic capabilities. Apparently, self-concepts of minority students cannot be based on perceptions. Self-concept is a self-descriptive behavior which can be observed, described, measured, and developed. I used this model in a 1992 project (Project Self-Responsibility) that resulted from a public service to schools. In this project, I developed and used *The 24 Open-Form Self-Concept Questions* to assess and enhance self-concepts of elementary students (in this case, predominantly African-American males who had been to jail for one reason or another). *The 24 Open-Form Self-Concept Questions* reflect self-knowledge, self-esteem and self-ideal.

The 24 Open-Form Self-Concept Questions

A. *Self-Knowledge Questions*

1. What is your name? Do you have other names?
2. What can you tell me about yourself, your classmates, your teachers and your parents?
3. How are you similar with your classmates?
4. How are you different from your classmates?
5. How "good" a student are you?
6. How "bad" a student are you?
7. How "happy" a student are you?
8. How well do you understand yourself?

B. *Self-Esteem Questions*

1. Which name do you prefer to be called? In other words, which name pleases you?
2. What are the things that you like best about yourself, your classmates, your teachers, and your parents?
3. Why do you like yourself for being who you are?
4. Why do you not like yourself for being who you are?
5. How do you like yourself for being similar with your classmates?
6. How do you like yourself for being different from your classmates?
7. Why do you think that you are proud of who you are?
8. Why are you happy (or maybe unhappy) because you love (or maybe hate) yourself for who you are?

C. *Self-Ideal Questions*

1. How did your understanding of yourself influence your school work?
2. How did your love for yourself influence your adjustment in school or how you relate to your peers?
3. How did your love for yourself influence your hard-work?
4. How has your understanding of your classmates, teachers, and parents influenced your academic success in school?
5. How have your similarities with your classmates affected your efforts?

6. How have your differences with your classmates affected your efforts?
7. What is your daily schedule? Do you know that "time is money?" What exciting or unexciting have you done today?
8. What was your high point this week? What was your low point this week? What have you learned about yourself that you are willing to change this week? What do you plan to change or accomplish next week?

The above questions encouraged African-American students who were at risk to take charge -- no response was viewed as wrong no matter how inappropriate. The results of Project Self-Responsibility are summarized as follows:

1. No African-American student involved in the project dropped out of school. One of the students in the elementary school progressed and moved into a regular classroom.

2. These African-American students started developing decision-making skills and began to take control of their problems.

3. These African-American students began to rely on their capabilities while acknowledging their weaknesses.

4. These African-American students understood they were responsible for their own feelings and actions.

5. These African-American students were able to realistically appreciate who they, their classmates, teachers and parents were.

As I indicated earlier, great teachers with great teaching techniques make multicultural teaching very simple. It is through building self-concepts that teachers could enhance peer acceptance and relations among all students, irrespective of their racial, cultural and linguistic backgrounds. In a multicultural classroom, teachers should care for all students. Caring teachers try to know their minority students. Caring helps minority students to *accurately* assess their capabilities as they relate to self-knowledge, self-esteem, and self-ideal. Caring should entail understanding minority students' strengths and using them to work on their weaknesses. Students who are not *appropriately* challenged are not well-cared for. Caring for minority students is not as simplistic as it traditionally means--it involves a combination of variables.

In a multicultural classroom, there are reasonable expectations for all students. Expectations lead to competency and sometimes to frustration (see Jawanza Kunjufu's 1984 book, *Developing Positive Self-Images and Discipline in Black Children*). It is important that teachers respect their minority students' learning styles. Like other students, they are different inter-individually and intra-individually. Appropriate expectations are more useful than lower or overtly higher expectations. Minority students need to be taught very early the importance of self-determination, self-respect and self-responsibility.

In a multicultural classroom, teachers listen to all their students. It makes it easy to discover where minority students are coming from when they are listened to. Good listening skills prevent self-hatred and enhance self-esteem. Cultural and family pride cannot take place without good listening. Poor listening can lead to alienation and deception; good listening brings teachers, parents and students together. If this is appropriately and consistently done, it is easy to observe personality changes in minority students. Supported children are inspired to be self-confident in whatever they set out to do. "Blind" support is as dangerous as "no" support at all.

In a multicultural classroom, all students are involved, and none is alienated. In all situations, minority students should be involved in making rules concerning their behavior. Teachers tend to take charge without involving all students they are supposed to help. Responsibility should not only come from teachers and other professionals; it should also come from students themselves. Self-concept cannot be enhanced without the personal involvement of the minority student in question. Self-involvement leads to intrinsic motivation and internal locus of control.

In summary, teachers need to understand that different students respond differently to different situations. Based on this premise, below are specific tips to guide teachers as they help minority students develop accurate self-concepts:

1. Learn to identify characteristics that help students understand who they are, what they value, and how to set and reach for realistic goals.

2. Create a school environment where students feel like an accepted part of the learning environment. Help them recognize when they are being productive and which behaviors best lead to school success.

3. Find and develop the students' intrinsic motivation that makes them aspire to work hard to reach their goals and take pride in their successes.

4. Emphasize that failing is not the end of the road, but a part of learning. Help students persevere by seeing the effort expended toward that task was good, but more effort is needed in order to succeed. Even though it hurts to fail, failure can be a motivation. Suffering breeds character.

5. Inspire students to learn how to control their lives. Encourage them to ask questions of themselves such as: What was the high or low point of the week? What did I change about myself or my life this week? What plans did I make for a future event this week? What do I plan to do, change, or accomplish for a future event this week? Also, involve students in setting disciplinary rules. This adds to their sense of controlling their lives.

6. Include feedback to students that show both strengths and, for the sake of making improvements, weaknesses.

7. Minimize reliance on global interpretations of test scores from instruments measuring self-concept.

8. Help students learn to set realistic goals. When minority students overestimate or underestimate their capabilities, they have difficulty establishing accurate self-concepts and setting realistic goals.

STEP SIX

Teach with Divergent Techniques

A disruptive student is no different from that same proverbial horse who would likely kick up his heels if he is held too long at the water when he isn't thirsty. Discipline is only a problem when students are forced into classes where they do not experience satisfaction. There are no discipline problems in any class where the students believe that if they make an effort to learn, they will gain some immediate satisfaction. To focus on discipline is to ignore the real problem: We will never be able to get students (or anyone else) to be in good order if, day after day, we try to force them to do what they do not find satisfying. If we insist on maintaining our traditional classroom structure, we will not be able to create classes that are significantly more satisfying than what we have now. (Glasser, 1986, p. 12)

We have grown with the idea that "things have to be difficult to be worthy." Teaching proves this statement wrong. For teaching to be successful, it has to be fun and students have to be able to relate to it (read Dr. Bob Algozzine's 1993 book, *50 Simple Ways to Make Teaching More Fun*). Many teaching situations in today's public schools could be handled differently. For successful multicultural teaching, the axiom should be "no one method of teaching answers all of our questions all the time." I was a member of a search committee to fill a special education position in one university. It was my duty to take the top applicant to lunch. In my discussion with this candidate (a White female), she indicated that she was a strict behaviorist since her major professors in college were behaviorists. I still remember vividly the contents of our conversation. I asked, "I appreciate your being a strict behaviorist. How can you teach a student who was still depressed because her cat died yesterday?" She responded, "What has the death of a cat got to do with classroom instruction?" I rephrased my question, "Let's assume that your student lost her grandmother who she loved so much. How would you handle it in your classroom assuming you had a test for all students?" She replied, "This student has to be ready for the test. What has the death of the grandmother got to do with the test that I have planned to conduct?" There was nothing wrong with this applicant's theoretical orientation; however, what is wrong is her failure to understand behaviorism and what it entails or her inability to apply other theoretical orientations in problem-solving situations when necessary.

Public school teachers are sometimes prepared by professors who have myopic ideas about other models of teaching. These teachers wind up using their *only technique* for all students year after year without respect for time, situation, trend and individual difference (see Dr. Thomas Lovitt's 1977 book, *In Spite of My Resistance. . . I've Learned From Children*). The students we teach today are of a different breed, and the old ways of doing things may not work. I am talking about change--we cannot just change for the sake of change. We have to change because there are many good reasons to change. Let's look at the statement below:

> The number of ads from the National Education Association tells us that the teaching profession is doing its job; it is not. We are not doing our best as a profession to tap the unlimited resources children bring into the classroom across the nation. The teaching profession has too many problems to devote its attention to the real job that is preparing our youth to compete and be leaders in a changing society . . . The profession will never take full blame for the lack of quality, lack of integrity and lack of ethics. It implies the false assumption that if children fail to learn, the fault must be with them rather than the schools. Yet schools that place the blame for students' failure on their "poor home environment" or "lack of motivation" do not hesitate to take credit when these same students succeed. Even our excuses are mediocre. We need to stop pointing to others. We are failing our children and ourselves. (Sullivan, Walko & DiSibio, 1990, p. 73)

All teachers do not lack integrity and ethics. However, some teachers have turned *politicians*. They blame students and their parents instead of devoting time and energy to doing what we do best, i.e., *teach*. We tend to forget that:

> Parents trying to raise respectful children today, unfortunately, have to do it in a disrespectful world. Brutal and hostile acts are shown in nightly television, profane, vulgar and irrelevant language is used routinely in the media; greed and selfishness are revealed in important and prominent people, role models are too outrageous or too perfect to be taken seriously. (O'Brien, 1991, p. 183)

Teaching is a rewarding profession when it focuses on "real pedagogical power." According to Dr. Asa Hilliard (1992), the Fuller E. Callaway Professor of George State University, Atlanta, Georgia:

> Real pedagogical power means that all children reach a high level of achievement on criterion-based standards. It means that all children who may have disabilities receive sophisticated, valid services that cause them to do better than they would have done if they had not received special services at all. (p. 168)

Education should have a positive impact on all students, their culture and race notwithstanding. The question is, "How" and "why" did "real pedagogical power" deteriorate or fail to accomplish its objective inspite of efforts through legislation and litigation. Again, we cannot legislate "real pedagogical power."

Dr. Jean Marc Itard, the French physician believed in "real pedagogical power" when he decided to take on the task of educating the "wild boy" of Aveyron, France in the late 18th century. Even the "wild boy" was able to acquire some appropriate skills. In the early part of the 20th century, Alfred Binet began to develop what is known today as the Stanford-Binet Intelligence Scale. He warned against excessive reliance on the intelligent quotient tool, yet we have continued to use it to quantify human intelligence. In speaking about his special class, Binet (1909) confirmed that intelligence of students can be improved through good teaching. He added, "It is in this parochial sense, the only one accessible to us, that we say that intelligence of these children has been increased. We have increased what constitutes the intelligence of a pupil: the capacity to learn and to assimilate instruction" (p. 104). In his book, *The Mismeasure of Man*, Dr. Stephen Jay Gould (1981) indicated that "if Binet's principles had been followed, and his tests consistently used as he intended, we would have been spared a major misuse of science in our century" (p. 155). The question is, Will this misuse of science continue in the 21st century? Today, freedom is abused, misinterpreted and misused. There is an apparent lack of ethics in classrooms, schools and communities. Troubled by this happening, Calabrese (1989) wrote:

> The failure to make ethics a priority has a direct impact on society in general and young people in particular. The school, as it continues to assume functions once formally held by the family has the potential and responsibility to train young people to act ethically. However, before schools can assume this function, they must view themselves as ethical

institutions and allow ethics to be the driving force behind all decisions and interpersonal actions. The demand to incorporate the teaching of ethics in schools should be consistent and equal to the demand to strengthen the academic program. (p. 39)

Teachers cannot continue to be slaves to theories and models of teaching. For successful multicultural teaching to take place, each theory or model should respond to the unique need of each individual student. I strongly believe the best teaching strategy is the strategy that works for a particular student at a particular time in a particular place by a particular teacher or service provider. Surprisingly, teachers are hired and/or fired because of their theoretical orientations. How, then, can teachers teach individual differences and diversity amongst students when they fail to accept divergent viewpoints by diverse people? Theories reflect conceptualizations and models, which in turn foreshadow interventions and pedagogy. Let's look at the following theoretical models:

1. Psychodynamic Model -- This model has evolved from the intrapsychic phenomenon espoused by Sigmund Freud. It is a connection of theoretical constructs which denotes an eclectic use of ideas and activities (e.g., the use of play, drama and art therapy to reduce inappropriate behaviors and enhance cultural diversity).

2. Biophysical Model -- This model emphasizes the organic origins of human behavior (e.g., the use of medical or biochemical techniques to remediate classroom behaviors).

3. Environmental Model -- This model connects the dominant theme in contemporary studies of human behaviors. Here, we find the sociological model (the way the society sees the individual) and ecological model (the way the individual interacts with the society) (e.g., the knowledge of environmental/home problems that impinge upon learning).

4. Humanistic Model -- This model is very student-centered. There is no structure and no judgement, and the focus is on sensitivity or empathy (e.g., incorporating sensitivity and active listening can enhance minority students' and parents' participation).

5. Behavioral Model -- This model discloses behavior changes that are observable and measurable (e.g., the use of behavior modification techniques can be reinforcing to minority students).

6. Cognitive Learning Model -- This model assumes that an individual's perception of environmental stimulus affects behavior changes. It is integrative in nature because humanism and behaviorism interface and interplay (e.g., the use of self-responsibility and Glasser's Reality Therapy can be effective in behavior management of minority students).

Based on these theoretical models, intervention and/or teaching strategies can be organized. These models reflect the divergent theoretical orientations that various professionals working with students in our public schools should use. For instance, when a teacher is a trained behaviorist, he/she cannot afford to downplay other strategies. Teachers should use other strategies to address needs of all students when problem situations arise. Since it is common knowledge that students' behaviors are complex, what sense does it make to use a simple approach to ameliorate a complex multidimensional problem? For some innovative answers, read Emporia State University's *Project Partnership's* 1994 handbook, *Competencies, Skills, and Knowledge Teacher Education Programs Need to Teach the Inclusion Teacher*.

In a multicultural classroom, divergent teaching techniques work. No one simple technique produces the best answer for all students. For further information, read the October/November Special Issue of *Exceptional Children* (Obiakor, Patton & Ford, 1992). In this Special Issue, Dr. Mary Franklin highlighted the following assumptions that undergird recommendations for culturally sensitive instructional practices:

1. Quality instruction should incorporate resources from the learner's environments outside the school parameters.
2. Special education should not be the primary solution for African-American learners whose cognitive and behavioral patterns are incompatible with schools' monocultural instructional methods.
3. African-American learners' differences should not be perceived as genetic deficiencies but, rather, as sources of strength.
4. Culturally sensitive teachers will identify and build on the learner's strengths and interests.
5. Language and dialectical differences are important cultural

influences that affect communication and interaction between the teacher and learner.

6. Culturally sensitive instruction should be integrated with activities that provide learners opportunities to learn and practice new skills. (pp. 116-117)

In addition, Dr. Franklin identified other specific teaching strategies for multicultural classroom instructions. These strategies include:

1. Stimulus variability.
2. Greater verve and rhythm.
3. Verbal interaction.
4. Divergent thinking.
5. Use of dialect.
6. Presenting real-world tasks.
7. Including a people focus.
8. Cooperative learning.
9. Peer/cross-age grouping.
10. Peer tutoring. (pp. 119-120)

These teaching techniques can work for all students. However, to get the best from minority students, these techniques have to be incorporated into instructional programs. Multicultural teaching encourages multidimensional techniques. I strongly believe we limit ourselves as teachers when we limit our teaching techniques. Additionally, as we limit our techniques, we limit our thinking. Minton and Schneider (1985) emphasized:

> We cannot limit ourselves to the identification of trait dimensions or topological classifications across individuals without also considering the characteristics of the environments within which individuals function. Nor can we limit ourselves to an analysis of the environmental determinants of human differences without also considering the hereditary determinants. Finally, we have to ask ourselves what kind of society is most desirable for the expression of human diversity - for the opportunity for each of us to grow as individuals and at the same time not infringe on the rights of others to develop their own individuality. (p.489)

We have been continuously bombarded with the phrase "effective teaching." It is time we started looking at effective teaching differently (see Dr. Howard Hill's 1989 book, *Effective Strategies for Teaching Minority Students*). Effective teaching should be characterized by an orderly school climate, a well-planned and implemented instruction, a concern for academic excellence, and high expectations for all students. In addition, effective teaching should incorporate "real" inclusive classrooms, schools, and communities. This means that effective teaching of all students must be fostered through collaboration, consultation, and partnership of all persons involved. Teacher preparation programs must respond to these ideals. They sometimes isolate themselves from real happenings in the society. Dr. Denise Roche (1990), the President of D'Youville College, Buffalo, New York, confirmed that:

> Often, educators are isolated from the real concerns of communities around them--it is not only important to teach others the knowledge and related skills necessary for their professional lives, but it is imperative that educators prepare graduates for specific areas of concern within their own communities and with the skills and motivation they will need to address them satisfactorily. (p. 32)

Dr. Carlos Diaz (1992) edited the book, *Multicultural Education for the 21st Century* which was published by the National Education Association. This book featured the "Who is who" in multicultural learning and teaching. Most ideas espoused by the authors are discussed below. Again, most great teachers will find it easy to implement these authors' ideas. My intent is to make teachers good teachers and good teachers great teachers. Let's not be defensive! If regular teachers had done the best job possible, we would not have had advocacies, litigations, and legislations to foster the education of atypical students. And, if special educators and other service providers had done the best job possible, we would not have had calls for inclusion, collaboration and partnership in our classrooms today.

Dr. Richardo Garcia (1992), a well-known scholar on multicultural learning and teaching, outlined a curricular blueprint that could enhance human rights and multicultural education in the classroom. He noted some assumptions needed by teachers interested in multicultural learning and teaching. They are as follows:

1.   All humans are members of one race, the human race.

2.   Humans exist as ends in themselves.
3.   Humans are ethically equal.
4.   Humans live in communities governed by natural laws and civil laws.
5.   Within the human society, for every right there exists a concurrent responsibility. (p. 173)

According to Dr. Garcia, a multicultural classroom should foster the right to exist, the right to liberty and the right to happiness. From his perspective, a classroom should be a physically safe learning environment where a teacher:

1.   Allows students to assert their opinions.
2.   Fosters respectful student dissension as a means for rational understanding of issues and divergent opinions.
3.   Enforces dress and hairstyle codes that allow for individual and group differences.
4.   Fosters examination of each student's ethnic or cultural heritage.
5.   Does not tease, ridicule, or demean students.
6.   Does not foster name calling or elitist, racist or sexist slurs.
7.   Does not reveal confidential documents, term papers, or notes to the whole class without the permission of the author.
8.   Does not reveal grades or remarks on class projects or term papers to the whole class without permission of the student.
9.   Disciplines students equally, insuring that minority students are not punished more severely than majority group students for same infractions.
10. Uses linguistically and culturally relevant curriculum materials and instructional strategies, telling students that their language and culture are welcome in the classroom community. (pp. 176-177)

Dr. Geneva Gay (1992), an authority in multicultural learning and teaching, outlined effective teaching practices for multicultural classrooms which include, but are not limited to the following:

1.   Using cooperative group, team, and pair arrangements for learning as the normative structure instead of as the occasional exception.
2.   Using learning stations, multimedia, and interactive video to present information instead of some form of lecturing.
3.   Varying the format of learning activities frequently to incorporate

more affective responses, motion, and movement.

4. Establishing friendships between students and teachers.
5. Creating genuine partnerships with students so that they are active participants in making decisions about how their learning experiences will occur and be evaluated.
6. Changing rules and procedures that govern life in the classroom so they reflect some of the codes of behavior and participation styles of culturally different students.
7. Devising ways for students to monitor and manage their own and each other's classroom behaviors.
8. Developing an esprit de corps of "family" to give cohesion and focusing meaning to interpersonal relationships in the classroom.
9. Including more human-centered and culturally different images, artifacts, experiences and incidents in classroom decorations and as props for teaching. (p. 53)

A multicultural classroom will be unsuccessful in a monocultural school community. The school community cannot afford to divorce itself from the goings-on in the classroom. The institutional climate is an integral part of what transpires in the classroom. Following are characteristics of successful school communities:

1. The school community engages in lengthy discussions about curriculum, organizational structure, assessment instruments, and educational purpose.
2. The school community believes in the ability of all students to succeed, and this vision permeates all areas of school.
3. Parents are participating partners in schools.
4. Teachers are involved in the decision-making process.
5. The principal is a key leader in guiding and directing the collective effort of the learning community.
6. Instruction is founded on developmental and social-skill needs of students.
7. Teachers consistently monitor and reinforce student academic performance. (Pang, 1992, p. 62)

Can you imagine a world without accountability? No classroom instruction is complete without an assessment, and no assessment is complete without initial instruction. We tend to think that assessment is divorced from instruction. This has been our traditional mentality and mistake. Assessment can be diagnostic (before instruction), formative (during instruction), and summative (after instruction). I indicated earlier that teachers and service providers have misused and abused tests. They have been used to quantify intelligence, categorize behavioral patterns of individuals and groups, and label people. However, tests can assist us to know, in some ways, how a particular student is responding to a particular instruction from a particular teacher at a particular time or situation. Multicultural education does not necessarily discredit all forms of assessment. It does advocate nondiscriminatory assessment that considers multidimensional variables. Drs. Ronald Samuda and John Lewis (1992) identified evaluation practices for the multicultural classroom which includes the following guidelines:

1. Diagnostic decisions, placement, and program changes in any counseling situation, should be based on a wide range of information about the student.
2. Assessment should result from a team deliberation on such information as how the student's performance is influenced by acculturation, language skills, behavior mode, socio-economic background, and ethnocultural identity.
3. The appraisal of the student's needs, strengths, weaknesses, and level of present cognitive functioning should be made with reference to the background data outlined in the previous guideline.
4. The main assessment objective should be to define and design a teaching or remedial program that would best help the student profit from the school system.
5. The remedial program should be carried out and monitored regularly by the assessment team. (pp.101-102)

My good friend and mentor, Dr. Bob Algozzine (1993), in his book, reiterated some facts about teaching. These facts can be borrowed by teachers of multicultural classrooms. As Dr. Algozzine pointed out:

1. You need to know the content you are teaching, and you learn a lot about teaching it by teaching it.
2. Teaching is the systematic presentation of instructional content, and you learn a lot about teaching by teaching.
3. Effective teachers plan, manage, deliver, and evaluate their

instructional content presentations.

4. Anybody can teach; people with very different credentials are successful at it and some of the best I have known have had training in academic content areas other than education.

5. Kids are the same all over. First grade teachers, second grade teachers, any grade teachers have problems. Gifted teachers have problems. Music teachers have problems. The only ones that don't are those who teach the severely and profoundly good.

6. Children come to school with needs. It is one of the teacher's jobs to meet them. Students come to school with problems. Teachers spend too much time worrying about and lamenting children's needs and it is easy to find someone to blame for the problems that students bring to class. If Johnny only came from a better home, teaching him would be so much easier. If Mary would get to sleep earlier, she'd be a better student. If Rachel's sister would treat her better, they would both be better off. The bottom line is: nobody ever got better just by knowing what was wrong. Teaching is an action-oriented profession. Time spent bemoaning causes of problems is time spent not teaching.

7. No class will be perfect. The best advice I ever gave anybody was this: take the class as it is, accept everybody in it, but expect them to change. (pp. 2-3)

Let's go back to my reason for writing this book. The teaching profession has great teachers and not-so-great teachers. Like many teachers, I love this profession. It surely hurts when a teacher who has little or no regard for *the codes of ethics of the teaching profession* is regarded as "a great teacher." Why can't respect for cultural diversity be included in teacher evaluation? My hunch is that we have graduated many teachers who chose teaching as their last resort. We have also seen universities graduate those who view teaching as a job for the "never-do-wells." Teaching is a profession for knowledgeable and caring people who not only love to teach but also believe education is a continuous process of growth. We need to reward excellent teachers who also have "hearts." Quality with "heart" is like "a house without a roof." Consider the following cases:

Case #13

Teacher A is a White female who has been teaching for many years. Because of her years of experience she was assigned to teach a particular class. She did not quite get along with one African-American male in her class. On one occasion, this student came late to class. He was wearing a pink shirt. Teacher A made fun of his pink shirt; and he got upset because his masculinity was challenged. He asked: "Teach, are you crazy? You didn't get enough last night?" Teacher A could not handle the insult and reported the student to the principal who did not hesitate to suspend him. She spent time in the teachers' lounge talking about the student's behavior and the kind of home he came from.

Case #14

Student A was the only minority student in her class. Her teacher (a White male) consistently made inferences on how she should have learned to function in the class. She had disagreed with her teacher's misinformation in English language, literature (poetry), history, and social studies. Even though this student performed very well in class, she was very uneasy. Because she was uneasy, her classmates started commenting that she needed to know how to "get along with others." Student A felt so uneasy that she transferred to another school that had many minority students.

Case #15

Student X was the only Black and minority student in his college statistics course. No other student wanted to sit around him. When he came late, he sat amidst the other students. After breaks, the other students moved to new seats away from him. He was treated like an outcast. He was very disgruntled that his teacher (a White male) did not care about what transpired in the classroom. His teacher gave group work but no one wanted to work with him. In the first test, he made the highest score and one of the few "A" grades. The teacher and students were surprised. After this test, these students wanted to sit around and talk with him. He refused to associate with them, and he was presumed "arrogant" by these same students.

Case #16

In a mainstreamed classroom of students with different capabilities, Student Y was the only minority student. Her teacher (a White female) incorporated achievements of minorities in her classes. On one occasion, Student Y had problems with addition and subtraction.

Everyone, including her teacher, knew that she loved basketball. To help her with her addition and subtraction problems, her teacher asked: "How many balls are used in a basketball game?" She responded: "One." The teacher asked: "If a team used six basketballs for warm-ups before a game, how many balls would be removed from the court before the game begins?" She responded: "Five." She was so happy and excited about learning that she began to teach her classmates who had similar problems.

A brief evaluation of these cases (Cases 13-16) demonstrates the need for using divergent techniques in teaching all students. In Case #13, the experienced teacher found it difficult to handle the student with slight inappropriate behavior. Her discussions in the teachers' lounge betrayed the student's right to confidentiality of information. She lost her cool, yet she did not expect the student to lose his cool. The student might not be the best behaved student in class; however, he could be having other problems outside the school. The teacher cannot afford to aggravate these problems with unnecessary jokes. Where was this student's right to due process? Where was the partnership between the school and parents? In Case #14, there was an apparent lack of sensitivity on the part of the student's teacher. One cannot assume that this teacher was racist. One can assume, however, that he lacked the skill needed for enhancing multicultural learning and teaching. He surely needed an in-service training, his years of experience notwithstanding. In Case #15, I was that student in the college statistics course. Many brilliant minority students find themselves in such situations. The teacher and students were not prepared for students like me. A logical extension is that White students need to be exposed to minority students who have gifts and talents. I had that experience in one of my graduate courses--the experience was both rewarding and educational. In Case #16, the teacher is well-versed on multicultural learning and teaching. She appears to know her students, their histories, values and symbols. She also appears to use divergent techniques to reach her students and stimulate their critical thinking skills.

As we have seen, no one simple technique works for all students at a particular time in a particular classroom. We must do what we can to teach students from divergent cultures using divergent techniques (read Dr. Eugene Garcia's 1994 book, *Understanding and Meeting the Challenge of Student Cultural Diversity*). We cannot afford the destruction of young minds. Our students are like our flowers--we have to nurture them so that they can grow and be productive, tax-paying individuals. The easiest route to eradicate "welfarism" is education that addresses multicultural needs of all students. We always remember those teachers who lit the candles in us. We also remember those who cursed our darkness. How can I forget those Peace Corps members who taught me English language, literature, French language and mathematics in Nigeria? I still remember how they looked--their vivacity touched us all. Is it any wonder that I wanted to come to the United States to study years later? Peace Corps programs have many advantages, e.g., multicultural learning and teaching. I encourage many White Americans to travel abroad and learn what it means to be *a minority in a majority culture*. We have many such programs in high schools and colleges. To foster multicultural learning and teaching, we must take advantage of such exchange programs. In his essay, "Experience of a Peacecorper," Dr. Kenneth Weaver (1994) of Emporia State University wrote:

> In December 1973, with a new B.S. degree in biology, I began a two-year service in rural public health in Santa Catalina, Negros Oriental, Philippines on the South China Sea. The conclusion of a conversation with myself in anticipation of the service's beginning was the observation that public health in the United States was probably without equal in the world. From this observation came a strategy for what was intended to increase my effectiveness—bring practices from home to the rural Philippines. For the first year, I lived according to this strategy. But public health is about bodily functions—waste disposal, reproduction, market sanitation, inoculation, and water purification. These personal topics are addressed when folks have a common frame of reference. How does one talk about waste disposal when there are no flush toilets? How can the potential sickness from the bacteria in a clear glass of water be explained to families who have used this water for generations? How can birth control be presented with no understanding of the cultural traditions of love, family, religion, or security? Thus, while the merits of my strategy to import home practices could be defended in theory, the result in practice was an "ugly American." Fortunately, the residents of Santa Catalina were a tolerant lot, but I suspect that quite a few folks were shaking their heads wondering who this strange American was and what he was doing here. An assessment of that first year produced only gloom. I was not happy; started projects were going nowhere; I had no friends, no buddies. Quitting was out of the

question; besides, the oil embargo, political troubles, and employment prospects in the United States made returning home less palatable. Fortunately, the stream of consciousness that produced such a dismal evaluation flowed to a precious point of illumination. I was a visitor in this country. It was not for me to come and through word and practice tell my hosts what to do. Rather, here was a wonderful opportunity for me to learn, and I was certain that these folks had plenty to teach me. That slight rearrangement of perspective irrevocably changed my life. Literally, the next day people started to invite me into their homes, to join them in their activities, to share a meal, and play with their children. And through these experiences, they taught me and changed me until I was able to pass on what I knew in a way that was harmonious to that culture. The last month of my service I finally was able to teach (after 23 months of my stay). Folks began to ask how they could prevent catching a particular sickness, what they might do to ensure their baby's health, how they might have fewer children, what kinds of food they might eat, what would happen if the town's garbage was dumped into the ocean, how does a vaccine work. So, what's the implication for multicultural education? *Plenty*! Knowing another culture is being intellectually alive, looking at the same reality from different viewpoints, having a vantage point from which strengths and shortcomings of one's own culture can be appreciated, elevating quality of life, enriching interactions with others, reveling in our commonalities, pondering our differences, and thinking of ideas never before considered. My experiences at Santa Catalina will remain with me forever. (pp. 1-2)

It is apparent that Dr. Weaver's multicultural experiences rub off on his students. It is our duty as teachers to encourage avenues of growth for our students. Great teachers find things that make students tick. My son's teacher was surprised when she asked about my son's interests--I told her that his interests are "cowboy" movies and soccer. She indicated that my son picked up those interests from me. "Not really! I love soccer and country music but not cowboy movies," I replied. By the way, my son calls them "cowmen" movies. To him, those men are not boys. I cannot convince him to call them "cowboys." He is correct. Yes, we can learn from children inspite of our resistance. For my daughter, her best television station is the TNN where she enjoys country music and dancing. We have shared these interests with their teachers. As parents, we have started using these interests to work on their disinterests. Teachers should do the same for all students. They have the tools to light the candles and not curse the darkness in their students. There are many techniques to light a candle--we can light it by sitting down, standing up, bending over, etc. The point is that there is much more fun to nurturing young minds than destroying them. The individual becomes guilt-free and garners self-gratification because he/she is enriching the human race. The people we teach hopefully will pick up our human qualities and share those qualities with the future generation.

In summary, no profession is more challenged in its job today than the teaching profession. I believe in the old African proverb, "it takes a whole village to raise a child." I also believe "the ignorant mind is the devil's work shop." The prescriptions I provided for teaching a multicultural classroom are not just from me. As we can see, I borrowed many ideas from different scholars and educators. Teachers should not be shy to borrow techniques that will assist them to reach their students. It is counterproductive for teachers to be tied to the apron string of one technique. Since we teach different students, it is logical that we use different techniques. Great teachers will find it easy to respond to this change--these teachers are great because they have consistently used divergent techniques to reach their students. Multicultural teaching techniques will add to the greatness of our classrooms. We need to try them not with tears but with smiles (see Dr. Crystal Kuykendall's 1992 book, *From Rage to Hope: Strategies for Reclaiming Black and Hispanic Students).* In the words of Dr. Kuykendall:

I am convinced that anyone who endeavors to develop children is a true hero/heroine. Not only do I believe in teachers, I revere them. I know how overwhelming the challenge of developing individuals can appear to be at times. But the real challenge is the challenge of commitment. When more teachers increase their commitment, and their repertoires of teaching techniques, more students will be able to succeed and more educators will reap the real joy this profession is capable of providing. (pp. 117-118)

STEP SEVEN

Make the Right Choices

Each person needs to learn to plan, to make wise choices, and to take responsibility for his/her life. Survival of our society, as a whole, requires that we learn how to plan wisely together. Moreover, it is clear that individually and collectively we need to improve in our ability to be self-directing and self-responsible-- and to have continuing faith in our ability to do so--if democracy itself is to survive. (Della-Dora & Blanchard, 1979, p. v)

The choices we make in life affect the decisions we make. By the same token, our decisions influence our choices. To a teacher, the important questions should be "Why did I become a teacher?" Do I have the characteristics that will make me a master teacher? Do I have the ability to bring out the best in my students? Do I have the capabilities to change my students to not only appreciate who they are but to also empower them to be functional decision-makers? Do I have the ability to make the right choices? These questions should arouse our judgements and stimulate our decisions.

I was faced with the choice of either going into business with my father or going into the teaching profession. I know I made the right choice to become a teacher. Since 1972 when I started teaching at Niblick Grammar School, Oghada, Bendel State, Nigeria, I have touched many lives, and many lives have touched me. When we make choices, we need to stand by them. That is why I strongly believe "we must look before we leap." The teaching profession has taken lots of punches (some of them rightly so). But if we are true-to-type and believe in what we believe, the teaching profession will get back its glory. Presumably, this is a tedious task. We have allowed politicians to define our profession. I have heard friends in other professions tell me that "I do not look like a teacher." How are teachers supposed to look? Depressed? Frustrated? Unintelligent? Teaching is my professional choice--I am obligated to make it the best. I had a friend who was pursuing his Ph.D. degree in Chemistry. He happened to fail his comprehensive examination. His major professors were very disappointed, but continued to support him. They suggested that he switch his major to Education with specialization in Chemistry. He registered for some higher level education courses. I suggested that he was making a wrong decision and that if those professors really cared for him, they needed to support his life-long dream of getting a terminal degree in Chemistry. To his surprise (not mine), he made very low grades in his education courses. He was amazed that he made very low grades. He had the preconceived notion that education was an easy major in college. In the general society, we find many people who have similar misconceptions about education. Try to tell someone you are a special educator! Automatically, you will get the person's sympathy. There is nothing more rewarding than having some knowledge and having the ability to use that knowledge.

This section of this book focuses on making the right choices. To make the right choices, teachers have to be knowledgeable about different educational models presented in this Step. The first model to be discussed is the "United States Interdependency Model" (USIM) which depicts the powerful nature of the United States in the world scene. We are fortunate to be citizens of the most powerful nation in the world. As citizens, our responsibilities are multidimensional. See Figure 1. As we can see, the United States depends on many countries for natural resources, and other countries depend on the United States for technical know-how and financial resources. Sometimes, we are fortunate to get military bases to further enhance our strength and place in the world. In our classroom instruction, we need to remind ourselves about our interdependency with other parts of the world--this broadens our vision and how we view the world. In other words, our knowledge of our interrelationship with other parts of the world will assist us in knowing who we are. We will ask less strange questions, and we will be less xenophobic about citizens of other countries who have immigrated or migrated to the United States.

The second model to be discussed is the "Multiethnic Model" (MM) which highlights the history, language, symbols, behavior, belief and event that people bring to the United States. See Figure 2. The early English settlers migrated to the United States to avoid dominance of the oligarchy of England. These migrants brought with them the Eurocentric method of education which has permeated our educational systems. As they settled, they began to formulate many principles which had many European strongholds. Native-Americans who were the first population in the United States had their beliefs which have been difficult to erase. Why would anyone want to erase another person's culture? Asians who migrated or immigrated to the United States have their linguistic and cultural differences. Hispanic-Americans also have their socio-linguistic and cultural backgrounds. African-Americans were brought as slaves to the United States from Africa. Other Africans have immigrated to this country. All Africans, regardless of how they came here, have brought to the United States different belief systems and cultural values.

The United States Interdependency Model (USIM)

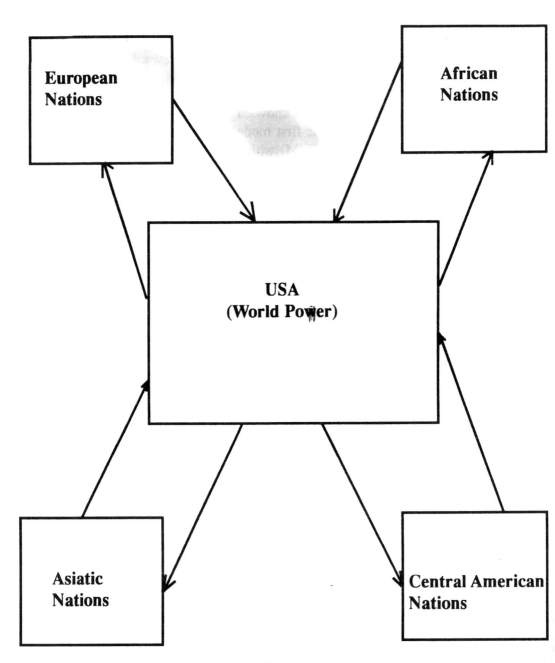

Figure 1

The Multiethnic Model (MM)

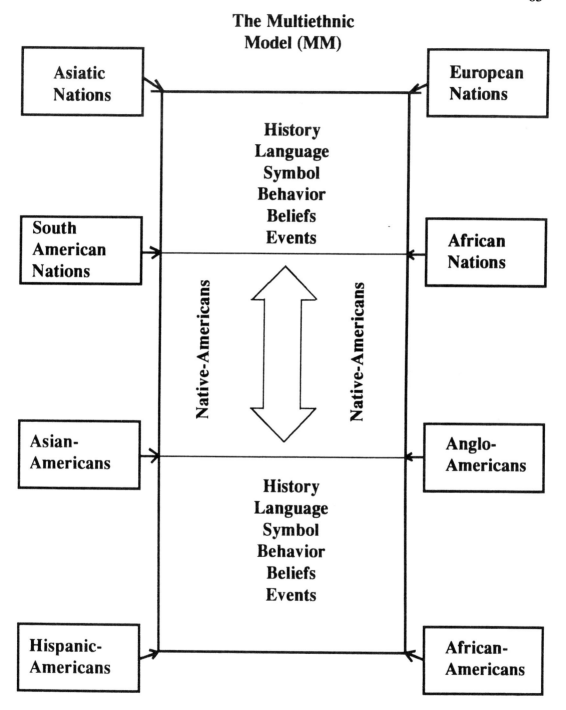

Figure 2

Teachers need to be knowledgeable about the multiethnic nature of the United States. Many cultures, values, beliefs and events have molded many Americans. All of these variables should be taught to students. It is baffling that our citizens are not very aware of these cultural variables. In fact, one culture is not better than another, only different. A better understanding of our relationship will make it easy for classrooms, schools and communities to be much more inclusive than we have been.

The third model is the "Inclusive Model" (IM) which indicates the role of collaboration, partnership and consultation in formulating good relationships among educators, parents and community leaders. See Figure 3. The inclusive model has a formula: 1C = MC + CC multiply by C + P + C. This means that multicultural classroom (MC) + cooperative classroom (CC) x collaboration (C) + partnership (P) + consultation (C) = inclusive classroom (IC). An inclusive classroom is a classroom that values cooperative learning and teaching. All service providers have to relate to each other with the student as the dominant person. It is not enough to say we care. We have to respect the strategic position of parents. Our expectations of them have to be those that will not alienate them or label them as individuals with deficits. Their values, cultures, beliefs and languages have to be respected. We cannot identify our students without their parents' involvement. We cannot test our students with total disregard for nondiscriminatory assessment. We have to be in constant touch with the students' parents so that they will be responsive when we invite them for meetings to arrange students' individualized education plans. When parents agree on these plans, they usually concur with placement options agreed upon by the team of service providers. It is almost self-destructive to try to intimidate parents who are our valuable resources, especially when students confront problems in school programs. Teachers facilitate instruction when there are good collaboration, partnership and consultation amongst educators, parents and other professionals involved with the student.

The fourth model to be discussed in this section is the "Teach-Reteach Modification Model" (TRMM). See Figure 4. As we can see, each new model is an extension of the previous model. For a multicultural instruction to flourish, the teacher should teach, modify instruction, teach, test, reteach, retest and teach again. This movement is cyclical and allows all students to be prepared to confront new learning and teaching. The global networks of multiethnic connections, inclusive interactions and modification efforts combine to make teaching more fun. They motivate teachers to be more prepared than before and to be more dedicated than other professionals in the delivery of services. Put another way, teachers and service providers have to provide

The Inclusive Model (IM)

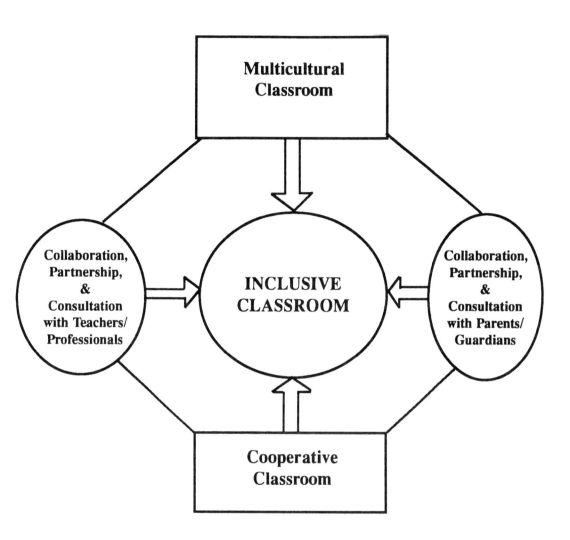

Formula: $1C = MC + CC \times C + P + C.$
   Inclusive Classroom (1C) = Multicultural, Classroom
   (MC) + Cooperative Classroom (CC) x
   Collaboration (C) + Partnership (P) + Consultation (C).

Figure 3

The Teach - Reteach Modification Model (TRMM)

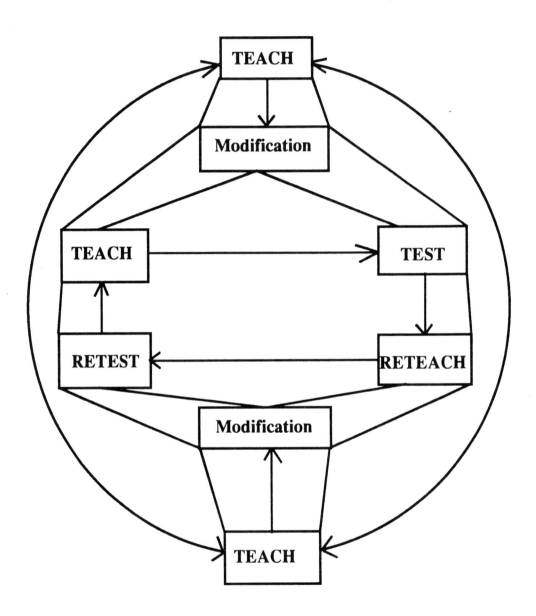

Figure 4

opportunities and choices for all students, their races, cultures and socio-economic backgrounds notwithstanding.

The fifth model that is discussed in this section is the "Opportunity and Choice Model" (OCM). See Figure 5. One major problem of multicultural learning and teaching is the lack of understanding of the impact of opportunities and choices. When opportunities and choices are created, education is provided at all levels. Minority communities need to commit themselves to self-respect, self-determination, self-survival, and realistic role models. These role models can be Whites or members of other minority groups. Multicultural education will be unsuccessful when minority group members fail to take advantage of opportunities and choices. These individuals have to be self-responsible. They cannot continue to drop out of school. They cannot continue to kill each other through gang wars. They cannot also continue to blame members of the dominant society for all the social ills confronting them. No individual can be free when he/she relies totally on government subsidies--this behavior leads to intellectual imprisonment and moral irresponsibility. We cannot advocate separatism while preaching cultural sensitivity and acceptance. I do not believe it is right to accuse Whites of Eurocentrism when, for example, African-Americans advocate Afrocentrism or when other Americans cannot gain employment in an area because they cannot speak the Spanish language. Minorities have to understand who they are, love themselves for who they are, and empower themselves for who they are. Self-knowledge is not enough--it must go with self-love and self-empowerment.

As we can see, the government is not divorced from the OCM. The OCM challenges the government to not give "deaf ears" to institutional racism. Schools, community businesses and state governments have to respond to this partnership. Civil rights of individuals must be taken seriously. Not long ago, a school principal (who happens to be an African-American) moved to Dubuque, Iowa to assume his position. Crosses were burned by members of a White supremacist organization in front of his house because they thought he moved into a wrong neighborhood. There was a national outcry in the media. The United States government must not condone such racial harassments. The Civil Rights Act of 1964 must be taken seriously by any citizen of this great country. Affirmative action regulations, though sometimes hard to regulate and unfair to some individuals, must be given their fair shake. These regulations have some dehumanizing effects on many minority administrators, teachers and students. As I indicated earlier, one of my former colleagues stated that my position at a university was a "desegregation" position, my hard-work and credentials notwithstanding. My hunch is that when we make efforts to

The Opportunity and Choice Model (OCM)

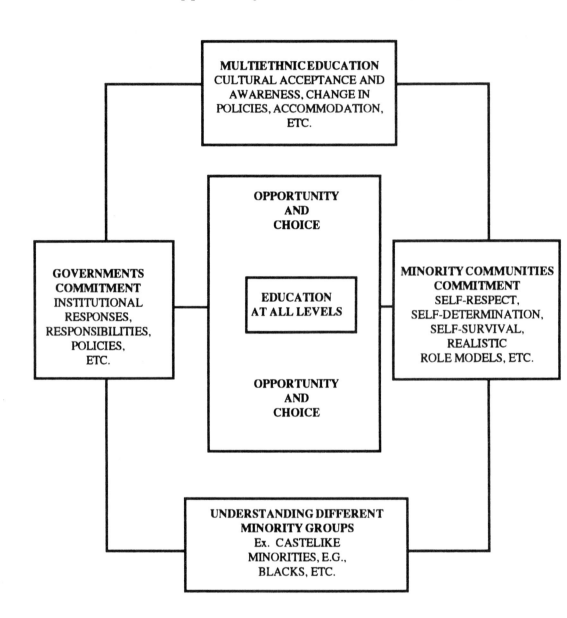

Figure 5

understand different minority groups, we begin to change our thinking and policies toward cultural acceptance, awareness and accommodation. As we have seen from the OCM, all hands must be on deck and efforts of all individuals are needed. Multicultural teaching cannot solely rest on the shoulders of Whites or minorities. It is neither a "White thing" nor a "minority thing." It must be an "universal thing."

The best method to provide opportunities and choices for minority students is to do whatever it takes to value and retain them in classroom, school, community, state and national programs. We cannot continue to allow minority and disadvantaged students to drift away and drop out of schools and programs that can make them productive human-beings in the society. The sixth model to be discussed in this section is the "Retention Model" (RM). See Figure 6. The Retention Model has four strategic phases which are absolutely necessary for multicultural learning and teaching to be properly fulfilled. Teachers must accept minority students. They should go further to acclimatize them to realities of classroom and school environments. The next phase will be to move them to be responsible individuals in classrooms, schools, and communities. These students should not just be satisfied with acceptance. Acceptance is a form of tokenism. Students should know what is going on in classrooms and be responsible for acquiring information covered in class. This means they have to go to classes, take notes, and study and remember what they have studied. They should take tests and pass them with excellent grades. Minority students should be prepared by teachers to be productive members of the classroom, school, community, state and nation. They should be taught to strive to be the best.

In the classroom, White students should be prepared to accept minority students. Teachers should use their instructions to foster peer relations and cultural acceptance. As students interact with each other, they should acclimatize each other with goings-on in schools and communities. Not long ago, an African-American male won a part in a local high school theatrical group. This high school senior was an excellent actor. In his role, he was supposed to marry one of his high school mates, a White female. Fearing reactions from the community, he was asked to play a subservient role. It was later learned that the parents of the girl did not appreciate their daughter marrying an African-American even though it was acting and unreal. This kind of retrogressive action destroys self-concepts of students and deters students from being responsible and productive.

Today, there are few minority teachers in our public schools. Our teacher education programs should endeavor to accept minority students and

The Retention Model (RM)

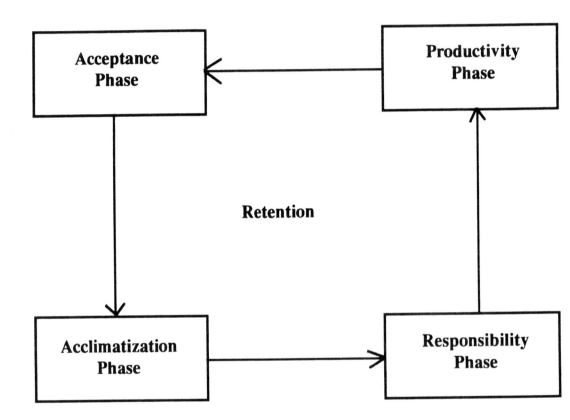

Figure 6

faculty and retain them to play productive parts in their programs. A former colleague was not happy when I indicated I was NOT fortunate to be the only African-American male in the teacher education program of a university. In his opinion, since that institution was a predominantly White university, I should have felt fortunate. In that teacher education program, mediocrity was the order of day. I was not learning and growing in that environment. I was the "Researcher of the Year" for two consecutive years, yet I should have felt fortunate to be around mediocrity because I am an African-American around White people. I learned very early that mediocrity had no racial, cultural or socio-economic boundaries. I was reminded of the Sidney Poitier movie, "Guess Who's Coming to Dinner?" where the White parent was surprised to see that the Black parent did not support the Black and White marriage. Many minority students and faculty are not satisfied with mere acceptance. The majority of them want to be "a part of the action." They want to be responsible and productive elements of the society in which they live.

The choices we make surely influence our actions. I am fortunate to have made the excellent choice of joining the teaching profession. I am happy about my decision. The question is, *Are all teachers happy that they chose the most rewarding profession in the world?* Teaching is one of the few professions that you can see what you have produced in less than one year, sometimes in one semester. Almost a decade ago, I was a guest speaker for a teacher's association. In the room, I saw many frustrated and depressed professionals who were not ready to confront changes and challenges of the 1990s. They asked questions that depicted self-hatred and great distaste for their profession. They raised issues about good salaries for teachers. In other words, they raised selfish issues that lend themselves to greediness and unethical behaviors. It is important we acknowledge that some teachers make more than some lawyers and other professionals. Teaching is not an inferior profession--some teachers have tried to make it an inferior profession. Lawyers defend their clients despite the gravity of their crimes. Medical doctors continuously treat their patients despite results of their diagnoses. Why can't teachers make such choices? We have to be proud of our profession and give people some reason to join us.

In summary, teachers need to be knowledgeable about the models presented in Step 7. It is a reality that the United States is a world power. As citizens of the greatest democracy in the world, we must be aware of our interdependency with the world. Our global knowledge is important--it will go a long way to reduce our ignorance and suppositions about other nations and people. Migration and immigration have served the United States well. Like our founding fathers, most people have migrated or immigrated with a set of beliefs, events, cultures, and symbols. The multiethnicity of the United States cannot be downplayed. Because of our multiethnicity, I advocate an inclusive classroom that incorporates multiculturalism, collaboration, consultation and partnership amongst teachers, service providers, professionals, parents and students. An inclusive classroom cannot survive without modifications in teaching and testing. Also, such a classroom cannot survive unless opportunities and choices for growth are provided for all students at all educational levels. In other words, the government must be involved, and minority communities must be involved. Institutional policies must be established to demonstrate respect for civil rights of all students. Efforts must be made to understand different minority groups--similar efforts must be made for cultural awareness and accommodation. We all must go beyond acceptance or mere tolerance. We must acclimatize students to the learning environment. We must make them responsible and productive persons in their learning and living environments. Consequently, we must encourage minority students to learn the right choices. We must make the right choices and convince these students at the same time to make the right choices. As we make our choices and provide opportunities for minority students, we must redefine what success means. According to Mr. Conrad N. Hilton (1987), the founder of Hilton Inn, in his book, *Be My Guest*, "To me there are ten ingredients which must be blended in each and everyone of us if we are to live successfully" (p. 279). These ten success-oriented ingredients are:

1. Finding our own particular talent.
2. Being "Big"--Thinking "Big," Acting "Big," Dreaming "Big."
3. Being honest.
4. Living with enthusiasm.
5. Not letting our possessions possess us.
6. Not worrying about our problems.
7. Not clinging to the past.
8. Looking up to people when we can and not looking down to no one.
9. Assuming our full share of responsibility for the world in which we live.
10. Praying consistently and confidently.

STEP EIGHT

Continue to Learn

Constant and uniform relations in change and a knowledge of
them in "laws," are not a hindrance to freedom, but a necessary
factor in coming to be effectively that which we have the
capacity to grow into. Social conditions interact with the
preferences of an individual (that are his or her individuality) in a
way favorable to actualizing freedom only when they develop
intelligence, not abstract knowledge and abstract thought, but
power of vision and reflection. For these take effect in making
preference, desire, and purpose more flexible, alert, and resolute.
Freedom has too long been thought of as indeterminant power
operating in a closed and ended world. In its reality, freedom is
a resolute will operating in a world in some respects
indeterminate, because open and moving toward a new future.
(Dewey, 1960, p. 287)

I strongly believe we never stop learning until we are dead. As I noted
earlier, some religions and cultures believe in life after death, i.e., even in
death, learning still continues. In any working relationship, people must
continue to learn about each other. We must believe education is a continuous
process of growth for multicultural learning and teaching to work. I still
remember my interaction with a business manager of one of the universities
that I attended. He was upset at me because I (a Black graduate assistant)
wanted a payroll deduction which he did for other White graduate assistants.
At the height of his frustration, he said, "Boy, get out of my office." When I
called him to task by writing to the Vice-President of Business Affairs, we
were asked to meet to resolve the conflict. I knew that this man needed to
learn more about multicultural education. His reasons for calling me a "Boy"
were interesting. First, he indicated he was not racist since he had many Black
tenants who live (and pay rent) in his houses. Second, he noted he did not
know I was a Ph.D. student. Third, he remarked he did not know the term
"Boy" was insulting even though he acknowledged he used it when he got
angry at his son. Fourth, he indicated he had a rough day and was not
particularly upset at me. His reasons might have been sincere; however, they
depicted some form of ignorance or inability to communicate. Let me state
emphatically that just having a minority as a friend does not necessarily mean

that one has learned all he/she must learn about multicultural education.

A few years ago, I was making copies from one of the photocopying machines in one university at which I worked. I saw a very cheerful White man--from his looks, he appeared wealthy and well-educated. He began a conversation with me, and said: "You are doing a wonderful job here. I went to the restroom and saw how clean it was. It was not that way when I went to school here many years ago." I was perplexed and responded: "Thank you, we try our best, but I am one of the college professors." He was also surprised, then he said: "Are you? I am sorry. Don't get me wrong? I have many Blacks who work for me." Again, I responded: "That's good, just remember that times are changing." It was apparent from my conversation with this man that he was presumptuous about me. The question is, Would he have misjudged my White colleagues as he misjudged me? There lies the crux of multicultural learning and teaching in today's classrooms, schools, universities and communities. We must continue to learn that times are changing or these times will consume us.

The big deal today is "political correctness" or PC which sounds like a response for insensitivity and lack of multicultural knowledge. While I detest the fact that we have to watch whatever we say, I strongly believe we cannot continue to destroy people's self-concepts by using free speech as an alibi. We must continue to learn how best to address the multiethnic nature of the United States. In addition, we must continue to learn how to reduce unwarranted generalizations, categorizations and stereotypic tendencies prevalent in our classrooms, schools, and communities. Parillo (1980) indicated that "portraying negative self-image as a fairly general tendency among minority group members, may be too broad a generalization" (p. 28). A few years later, Arciniega (1986) warned against the dangerous presumption that poor and minority students are "culturally deprived" or "disadvantaged." These negative assumptions are frequently internalized by minority students--they are forced to deal with the negative influence of the self-fulfilling prophecy. For further reading, see Dr. Nell Irvin Painter's article "It's Time to Acknowledge the Damage Inflicted by Intolerance" published in the March 23, 1994 issue of *The Chronicle of Higher Education*. PC or no PC, respect and responsibility must prevail.

I strongly believe "a good teacher should be a good student." There are many advantages about learning to learn, experiencing learning and experimenting with new learning. The more we learn, the less we make unwarranted presumptions about individuals, groups, races, religions, genders, skin colors and nations (see Drs. Phyllis Katz and Dalamas Taylor's 1988 book, *Eliminating Racism*). There is no philosophy that answers all of our questions; however, the more pragmatic we are, the better. Events, situations and life are fluid--they are not genetically handed down. They are multidimensional; they change depending on contexts and they must never be based on perceptions and presumptions. When it comes to understanding human behaviors and phenomena, "what you do not know usually hurts you." Life is complex--it is not a question of "yes" or "no" since it involves complex human behaviors and phenomena.

Bronowski (1971), in his book, *The Identity of Man*, emphasized that human animals learn from experience, and because of their ability to engage in abstract thinking, they are different from other animals and machines. Today, much talk is about "information highways." I support these "information highways." However, we must make sure that they do not take away from our human thinking. The human is an insecure animal--we do not want to go into seclusion. The more people interact with each other, the more we learn about each other. I have had colleagues who could have cared less about human relations, faculty meetings, and committee works because they were consumed by their computers. I pray that these "information highways" do not take us away from selecting answers to basic problems of ontology (problems of being), epistemology (problems of knowledge), and etiology (problems of value). In his book, *Human Nature, Animal Nature: The Biology of Human Behavior*, Cohen (1975) noted that human animals are a troubled species--they are highly intelligent, yet often do stupid and dangerous things. As teachers, we must continue to ask two important questions. How can any social system be changed without changing the general machinery of that system? How can the general machinery be changed without appropriate changes in the philosophy of education? We need technologies and computers. I just hope they do not do our thinking for us. We need problem-solvers. Our society is changing as our demographics are changing. My hunch is that our social system cannot change until our educational system is changed to suit our cultural, societal, political and economic needs.

As we continue to learn, our philosophies about life continue to change. See Figure 7 for the "Philosophical Model" (PM). It is always disheartening when I see teachers who refuse to attend in-service trainings or professional conferences. As teachers, it is important that we belong to professional organizations and continue to learn of improvements. Since 1990, most professional organizations have focused their conference themes on "cultural diversity." I am very sure that members of these organizations are not playing games--they are trying to address "real" problems of "real" people. About half

The Philosophical Model (PM)

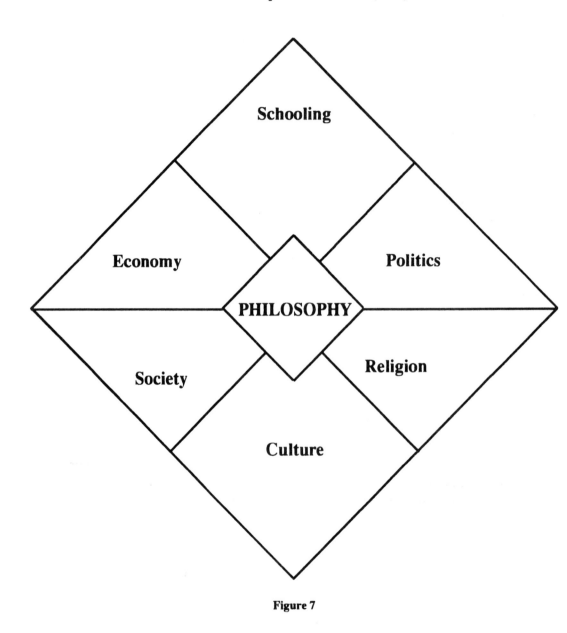

Figure 7

a century ago, Myers and Williams (1954) in their book, *Education in a Democracy* argued that "the main bulwark of a democracy is an informed and intelligent citizenry, trained in active participation in government" (p. 192). I must say this is difficult in societies with high levels of illiteracy, tribal, racial or religious problems, and dictatorships. As Bronowski (1971) pointed out, "Each man (or woman) has a self, and enlarges his (or her) self by his (or her) experiences. That is, he (or she) learns from experience: from the experiences of others as well as his (or her) own, and from their inner experiences as well as their outer" (p. 77). All human-beings must be involved in the process of learning. Dr. Julius Nyerere (1985), a well-known philosopher and former President of Tanzania, East Africa wrote in the *Harvard Educational Review*:

> Education is not something which is done just in schools. The process of education begins to shape the children before they ever enter a classroom. Education starts in the home at the time of a child's birth and continues as the child grows up in the local community... Formal education is bound to be--and from society's point of view is intended to be--an element in maintaining or developing the social, political, and economic culture of that society. (p. 45)

It is obvious that no democracy can operate in an ignorant society. Dynamic education must be the basis for restructuring and formulating a new society. More than two decades ago, Mayer (1973) in his book, *Education for a New Society*, explained that "from kindergarten to graduate school a cosmopolitan perspective should prevail, so that the distant needs become immediate responsibilities" (p. 33). Multicultural education demonstrates dynamism in education. It fosters our understanding, acceptance and value of who we are and of people around us. It has been predicted that in the year 2000, the world will contain about 6.4 billion people. A tremendous increase over today's population, and a great proportion will not be White Anglo-Saxon Protestants (WASP). A logical extension is that the more we understand these different peoples and cultures, the easier it is for us to restructure and reframe our strategies world-wide.

Our world is getting "smaller"--Europe is uniting (e.g., the one currency agreement) and the Americas are trying to unite (e.g., the North America Free Trade Agreement). Teachers must continue to learn and teach the implications of global restructuring movements. How can we trade with other people without understanding their languages, cultures and symbols? How can we be the greatest democracy in the world when our school programs fail to emphasize the importance of the individual, social responsibility, the right to self-government, freedom and liberty? As I have indicated, learning should not be a "White thing" or "minority thing;" it should be an "universal thing."

Violence, gang wars and drug abuse are rampant in today's society. Continuous learning is the key. Why should an African-American kill another African-American and blame it on the White person? Why should "babies" have babies and blame it on the society? Why should someone abuse drugs because a friend abuses drugs? Without multicultural learning and teaching, how can we teach minorities that all Whites are not racist? How can we also teach Whites that all minorities are not social burdens? We need to understand that multicultural learning and teaching benefit all persons, groups, genders, religions, races and nations. We cannot continue to live "in the dark." The media must be very involved. We cannot also continue to negatively present some individuals as "poor," some schools as "poor," some groups as "poor," and some communities as "poor." It is counterproductive to project certain individuals, groups and communities as less Americans or less patriotic than others because of their views and behaviors. The retired Chairman of the Joint Chiefs of Staff of the United States Military, General Colin Powell, is an African-American whose parents migrated to the United States from Jamaica, West Indies. There are many great minds from all cultures and races. We must continue to learn and teach that giftedness goes beyond racial, cultural, and socio-economic lines. We limit ourselves and our options when we stop learning about other individuals and groups. It is no wonder I feel demoralized when I am told that I do not act like an African or a Black. Our skin color should be a part of our pride. There is nothing wrong in being White. In fact, I love the White culture. In the same dimension, I love the African-American culture, Hispanic-American culture, Asian-American culture and Native-American culture. The question is, How can an individual love (or dislike) "what" or "who" he/she does not know? As teachers, we must continue to learn and teach about different cultures using different techniques. When we stop to learn and teach, we stop to appreciate and value our beauties and the beauties of others.

Let's not kid ourselves! There is so much to learn about classroom instructions, school programs and community living, especially now that our demographics are rapidly changing. If we had learned and taught all the right things, we would not be having discussions today on how we can shape our educational and social future. Also, if we had learned and taught all the right things, we would not be talking today about the multidimensional problems that minorities experience in our classrooms, schools and communities. As we can see, these problems include (a) the misleading theory of "biological determinism" which subscribes to the principle that "worth can be assigned to individuals and groups by measuring intelligence as a single quantity" (Gould, 1981, p. 20); (b) the misuse of standardized instruments for inappropriate classification, categorization, and placement (Anrig, 1985; Hilliard, 1989; Obiakor, Algozzine & Ford, 1993; Samuda, 1975); (c) the unproductive global/perceptual assumption that minorities have "low" or "negative" self-concept because some experience failures in school programs (Obiakor, 1992b); (d) the insufficiency of realistic role models (e.g., minority teachers) who understand their history, symbols, cultural values, and learning styles (AACTE, 1988; Algozzine & Obiakor, in press; Harvey & Scott-Jones, 1985; Ogbu, 1988, 1990; Staples, 1984); and (e) the lack of multiethnic education to foster cultural acceptance and diversity (Bank, 1977, 1992, 1994; Gay, 1975, 1992).

We must continue to learn reasons for litigation and legislation in education. Our knowledge of our past will help us to know our present and predict our future. We must refrain from making old mistakes. We have to learn that the quest for higher test scores legitimizes the monocultural mentality which the 1954 *Brown versus State Board of Education* at Topeka, Kansas case sought to combat. We also have to learn that other legal and legislative efforts have been made to combat unidimensionality in education and meet the needs of all individuals, irrespective of race, color, gender or national origin. They include, but are not limited to (a) the 1964 Civil Rights Act, (b) the 1965 Elementary and Secondary Education Act (ESEA), (c) the 1970 *Diana versus California School Board* case, (d) the 1972 *Miller versus Board of Education*, Washington D.C. case, (e) the 1973 Section 504 of the Vocational Rehabilitation Act (Public Law 93-112), (f) the 1975 Education of All Handicapped Students Act (Public Law 94-142), (g) the 1990 Americans with Disabilities Act (Public Law 101-336), and (h) the 1990 Individuals with Disabilities Education Act (Public Law 101-476). These laws and court cases did not happen by accident or in vain. I do not believe we can legislate "love" and "sense of caring." However, for us to prescribe treatments and antidotes, we have to learn about our diseases.

We must continue to learn why we have an underrepresentation of minorities in gifted programs and an overrepresentation of minorities in special education programs. For further reading, see Drs. Alfredo Artiles and Stanley Trent's 1994 article in volume 27, number 4 of *The Journal of Special Education* where they addressed the issue of overrepresentation of minority students in special education. A few years ago, Rev. Jesse Jackson (1988), the

President of the Rainbow Coalition and founder and past President of
Operation PUSH, listed problems of the African-American minority group in
the educational system. They include, but are not limited to the following:

1. Loss of teaching and administrative jobs by Blacks through
    dismissals, demotions, or displacement.
2. Loss of racial models, heroes, and authority figures for Black
    children.
3. Loss of cherished school symbols, problems, and names of schools
    by Black children when their schools were closed and they were
    shifted to White schools.
4. Subjection to segregated classes and buses, and exclusion from
    extracurricular activities.
5. Suspension and expulsion of disproportionate numbers of Black
    students.
6. Exposure of Black children to hostile attitudes and behavior of
    White teachers and parents.
7. Victimization by forced one-way busing policies and the
    uprooting of Black children for placement in hostile school
    environments.
8. Victimization by misclassification in special education classes
    and tracking systems.
9. Victimization by unfair discipline practices and arbitrary
    school rules and regulations.
10. Victimization by ignorance of Black children's learning styles
    and cultural, social, educational, and psychological needs. (p.
    455)

Rev. Jackson might sound very political; however, the problems he identified
are very real. We must continue to learn how to provide treatments and
antidotes for minorities. As Algozzine, Maheedy, Sacca, O'Shea and O'Shea
(1990) pointed out, "We are not convinced that the cause of our field's
condition is so promising that we cannot freely offer any medicine, even those
available without prescriptions that may not as yet be doctor-tested" (p. 556).

We must continue to learn about our students and our world. In his book,
Multiethnic Education: Practices and Promises, Dr. James Banks (1977)
affirmed that:

We live in a world society beset with momentous social and human

problems, many of which are related to ethnic hostility and conflict.
Effective solutions to these critical problems can be found only by
an active, compassionate, and ethnically sensitive citizenry capable
of making sound decision that will benefit our ethnically diverse
world community. (p. 32)

A logical extension of Dr. Banks' statement is that teachers must continue to
learn (a) historical backgrounds of their minority students, (b) languages and
symbols that minority students bring to class, (c) behavioral patterns of
minority students, and (d) events which have molded minority group members.
Education should not be viewed simplistically as a White peoples'
prerogative--it should be associated with democracy and "real" freedom for *all*
Americans. Dr. Manning Marable (1990), Chair of African-American Studies
at Columbia University, New York, alluded to this notion when he argued:

If the curriculum of our public schools does not present the heritage,
culture and history of African-Americans, if it ignores or
downgrades our vital contributions for a more democratic society,
our children are robbed of their heritage. They acquire a distorted
perspective about themselves and their communities. If they believe
African-American people have never achieved greatness, in the
sciences, art, music, economics and the law, how can they excel or
achieve for themselves? (p. 5A)

We must continue to learn what our present and future challenges are.
According to Dr. Marable (1993):

Our challenge is to revive the ideal of education, by forging to
conditions in our school systems and national educational policies, to
advance the promise of new levels of excellence. Unless we
accomplish this, our country lurches toward an inevitable crisis
between the affluent, educated "haves" and the uneducated, barely
alienated "have-nots." The choice is ours, and the time is short. (p.
5A)

We must continue to learn about multicultural education not because we
are scared of some inevitable crisis or consequence, but because it is the right
thing to do. I do not believe our world is coming to an end--I believe in
appreciating the beauties of life. We have to learn to appreciate these beauties.

When I accepted my new position at Emporia State University, some friends were worried because of the low representation of minorities in Kansas classrooms, schools and communities. I was told that Kansas is a conservative state. Based on measurable data, it is apparent to me that this might be one of the finest decisions I have made in my life. I have learned a lot since coming to Emporia--most of my experiences have been rewarding. I am the only Black male in my Division and College--I have been treated with more respect than what I received when I was in colleges, cities and states with more Blacks and minorities. I have continued to learn we cannot generalize that Democrats or Republicans are "bad" or "good." We have to relate to individuals area-specifically and situation-specifically. We must desist from categorizing and labeling people, events and situations.

As I indicated earlier, I was the only Black or minority in three courses that I taught in Fall 1993. I could see the uneasiness in the faces of my students. Even though I have had many years of college teaching experience, I wanted to understand my students. To reach them, I had to try divergent techniques. During the process, I had to appreciate their individualities and put into practice divergent classroom techniques which include:

1. Explaining fully what was expected of my students.

2. Giving praise freely to students when it was earned.

3. Presenting students with correct answers or methods first.

4. Teaching students by example.

5. Disciplining students without humiliating them.

6. Providing students with constructive activities to replace ones I wanted to inhibit.

7. Using concrete objects for demonstrations to my students.

8. Progressing to more difficult tasks when simpler tasks were mastered by students.

9. Creating students' interests and attention.

10. Spelling for students difficult-to-understand words because of my accent.

11. Structuring my students' classroom environment.

12. Giving students choices whenever possible and following through.

13. Encouraging students' attempts to perform a task.

14. Smiling a lot and reminding my students about the beauties of the teaching profession and life.

15. Using personal experiences in teaching to stimulate students' critical thinking and problem-solving skills.

16. Using "ladies and gentlemen" to refer to my students.

17. Focusing on outcomes or what students have learned and not on tests.

18. Helping my students to continuously search for "new" meaning as we explore "new" learning.

19. Providing universal themes while responding to my students' unique needs.

20. Evaluating my students' growth in more ways than one.

Some of my students were initially leery--for many of them, I was the first Black or minority to have taught them. I did not give up--I continued to learn how to reach them. During the Fall 1993 semester, one of my White male students wrote two poems (unpublished at the time) titled, "Happiness" and "Friends Forever." He wanted to let me know how much I touched him. Here are the two poems!

Happiness
By John Rahija

Happiness is a thing called life

It bears many fruits
To live and die and sacrifice
the sorrow, pains, and truths.

Happiness is a seed of giving
A fate to be cherished and held
The more you give, the less you take
is what happiness does well.

Happiness makes you proud
of maximizing a person's success
To achieve your goals
is what happiness does best.

To be happy is to be grateful
for all the things in life
The surprises, tears, and dramatic fears
that cut through life like a knife.

Happiness is all the experiences
that one struggles in life
Good or bad or maybe sad
without happiness there is no life.

Friends Forever
By John Rahija

I'd like to say I'm sorry friend
for how I treated you in the past.
Forgive me for the things I said
and let our friendship last.

I hoped we could still be friends
this is why I wrote this poem.
Since you are very dear to me
let's keep the friendship goin'.

Let's not depart or tear apart
the friendship we once had.

For I am blue and lonely too
without you I am sad.

If there is something I can do
to make a wrong a right.
Talk to me, let me know
morning, noon, or night.

It's my request, I'll do my best
to be gentle, friendly, and kind.
Most of all I'll perfectly dissolve
the past which now is behind.

During this period, there was a White male graduate student who I discovered with lots of potential. It has always been my belief that I am a role model to all students inspite of their race, culture, color, religion, gender, sexual orientation and national origin. For us to avoid paradigm paralysis, we must learn to be role models not just to people of our own race but also to people of other races and cultures. On this basis, I invited this student to speak in my undergraduate class on a topic he so passionately loves, i.e., "The Memorable Debate between B.F. Skinner and Carl Rogers: Classroom Implications." He did a wonderful job! I sent him a letter of thanks for speaking in my class and took him to lunch several times during the semester. Below is his September 29, 1993 response to my letter.

Dear Dr. Obiakor:

Thank you very much for providing me the opportunity to come speak to your class on Wednesday. I really enjoyed lecturing to an upper level special education class. It was particularly interesting to note the differences between your class and mine.

I believe in the power of the spoken word, but I also believe the written word is equally important. It kind of ties everything together. "Keep your eyes on the prize," you have said. That is some of the best advice someone has ever given me. Thank you for that, too.

I look forward to getting to know you better and working with you in the future. Let me know if I can be of any help.

David S. Weintraub.

Presently, David loves graduate school; and he is very motivated to complete his Master's degree and pursue his Ph.D. degree. If David had been an African-American, a Native-American, an Asian-American or an Hispanic-American, I would have done the same thing. It is not impossible for teachers and professionals working with minority students to treat them the way I treated (and will continue to treat) David. We have to continue to learn how to reach out and touch them. We cannot afford to have a different set of informal rules for minority faculty, staff, and students. We seem to be more concerned with higher test scores in teacher education programs than what we can do to motivate students to be great teachers and great human-beings.

I indicated earlier that I am the only Black male in my Division and College. However, I am convinced that I made the best decision to accept my position. I have great colleagues--they are proactive on multicultural issues. Our Teachers College has different focus group discussions which include the "Multicultural Focus Group" and the "Great Books Focus Group." The Multicultural Focus Group engineers discussions on "how minority students and faculty are treated on campus" in respective departments and divisions. Interestingly, the chairperson of these Focus Groups is a White male. In the Great Books Focus Group, we read and discussed the educational implications of Jonathan Kozol's book, *Savage Inequalities* and Dr. Victor Frankl's book, *Man's Search for Meaning.* I have been impressed with the dedication and commitment of members of these focus groups. As a member of the Great Book Focus Group, the Dean (a White male) had encouraged the establishment of these focus groups as a faculty development process. Apparently, this Dean knows and believes we must continue to learn. This same Dean is one of the few Deans who has not patronized or paternalized me, a behavior we see everyday in workplaces where we have minorities. In his Spring 1994 address to the Teachers' College faculty and staff, this visionary Dean outlined his priorities to include (1) diversity among faculty, staff and students, (2) quality instruction, (3) technological advancement, (4) program evaluation and modification, (5) faculty development, and (6) response to students' needs. Also, in the Spring semester, the Vice President for Academic Affairs and the President of the University did not mince words when they addressed the issue of diversity of faculty, staff and students. Clearly, embedded in these presentations were visionary issues that would make our university programs competitive in the 21st century.

In one of the universities at which I worked, there were many administrators who talked so much about "excellence" and "quality" in education with total disregard for "equity." In that university, games were played with students' evaluation of faculty to the extent that mediocrity became the order of the day. Teachers gave undeserved "As" to students so that they would rate them as "great" teachers. These teachers were not encouraged to learn, and they never attended professional conferences. In that environment, negativism was encouraged as a personal idiosyncracy. People were not judged on productivity--they were judged on "likeness" and "who you know," both unmeasurable variables. Today, I see many schools and universities floundering in mediocrity in an effort to keep the status quo. They pay lip service to quality and refuse to address diversity as a reality. In fact, they see the issue of diversity in classrooms, schools, and universities as a "game" or controversy that will soon be over. Multiculturalism is not a game. Teacher education programs must learn to appreciate and value diversity.

Since diversity is a nontraditional phenomenon, we must continue to learn new proactive methods. We cannot continue to be reactive--we cannot also continue to blame others instead of assuming responsibilities. Put another way, we cannot continue to pretend that we know all we need to know about multicultural education. In my present university, multicultural issues have not been swept under the rug. This institution understands the importance of introducing multicultural education into our classroom instruction, school programs, and community interactions. For instance, my colleagues involve me in their projects, and I involve them in mine. My impression is that they have tried to understand me, and this has made it easy for me to relate to them. We consistently hear how minorities fit or do not fit into the team in most workplaces. We never hear how the team attempts to fit into the needs of minorities. It appears that my colleagues and students prepared themselves for my entry into the team. Again, this made it easy for me to quickly adjust into the team. As we can see, the burden of proof on collegial relationship is not placed on me alone. Everyone is involved in the cultural partnership, collaboration, and teamwork.

My positive experiences in my present university have several implications for multicultural learning and teaching. First, cultural learning is a continuous process of growth. Second, cultural team-work can be achieved when people work together. Third, when we reach out to culturally different people, there is a high probability that they will respond. Fourth, multicultural learning and teaching are not impossible in classroom, school, and university programs. Fifth, when educational programs are made to fit the needs of minority faculty, staff, students, and families, they enhance quality--they do not lower quality (Obiakor, 1993; Obiakor & Barker, 1993). Put another way, multicultural education can be achieved when we open our minds to "new" knowledge. We cannot achieve multicultural environments when we categorize people or when we refuse to change our negative perceptions. It was apparent that I did not want to narrow my options, and neither should anyone. I would have narrowed my options if I had rejected my position because Kansas does not have a large African-American or minority population. I am even more convinced today than before that I am not just a role model to African-Americans; I am also a role model to Anglo-Americans, Native-Americans, Asian-Americans, and Hispanic-Americans.

It is important that we continue to embrace "new" knowledge. Most of the "new" knowledge are "old" knowledge which we previously failed to embrace. Minority students have unique needs which cannot be downplayed or downgraded. Teachers must continue to learn the meaning of the phrase "curriculum relevance," i.e., the curriculum that connects the affective or feeling aspect. This combination is what Castillo (1974) called "confluent education," an education which promotes the interaction between intellectual, emotional, and physical learning. Teachers must continue to learn how to improve knowledge, thinking, attitudes, and skills. We must understand that knowledge does not automatically produce a way of thinking and that attitudes can best be developed through confrontation with experiences and materials which impact on feelings. For further information, read Drs. Judy Pearson and Paul Nelson's 1982 book, *Understanding and Sharing*.

Dr. Geneva Gay (1975) acknowledged that there are economic, psycho-social, and eco-political issues that are pertinent to various ethnic groups. Teachers must continue to learn that the many dimensions of lives of ethnic group members include (a) cultural characteristics, (b) inter-group variations, (c) their present status in the society, (d) conditions of their political, economic, and social existence of historical perspectives, and (e) their contributions to the development of the American culture and of human-kind. It is imperative ethnic content become an integral part of all fundamental educational experiences, and a regular feature of daily curriculum, instead of reserved for special units, courses, and occasions. Learning and teaching must be viewed from ecological contexts. We must continue to learn how to make our curricula culturally relevant based on our personalities, experiences, attitudes, and expectations.

Teachers and service providers cannot expect miracles happen on their own in their classrooms and school programs. They have to make those miracles happen. No longer must teachers and other professionals continue to nurture the "get rid of" minorities (or any other student) attitude. Mr. Robert De Bruyn (1984) in his publication, *The Master Teacher*, agreed that:

> If we adopt a "get rid of" attitude, we violate a basic tenet of education: that each student is an individual, and that our instruction and curriculum must try to make allowances for individual differences. Regardless of our feelings, we cannot discount this tenet. That's why it's dangerous to adopt a practice that amounts to saying, "Get the uninterested, unmotivated, and ill-behaved out of the school to keep them from interfering with those who want to learn." In truth, this is an easy way out. And teaching all students is not easy. Yet, it remains our challenge. (p. 1)

On March 17, 1994, a colleague (Dr. John Agada) and I delivered a paper titled, "The Politics of Education: Imperatives for African-American Males in the 21st Century" at the 22nd Annual National Association for Ethnic Studies (NAES) Conference held in Kansas City, Missouri. Issues raised by Mr. DeBruyn on the preceding paragraph became our central theme; and based on this theme, we proposed a Comprehensive Support Model (CSM). See Figure 8. The CSM will work for other minority students and many at-risk White students. From this premise, the home has a role to play, the school has a role to play, and the society has a role to play. Minority students need to know they can go to school and be valued in school. They also need to know they can maximize their potential, graduate and get jobs. Educators should intrinsically motivate minority students to begin to engage in purposeful change which could lead to a purposeful life.

I strongly believe with an excellent connection of the support base, minority students would acknowledge that failure is not the end of the road. This support base must help them to assess and reassess each situation area-specifically so that they do not categorize all classroom problems as "racism." To achieve goals, some objectives (or in this case preparations) are needed. These preparations must be observable, measurable, specific and action-oriented. It is unrealistic to expect a minority student to succeed in educational programs without an accurate knowledge of "self," a strong and supportive parent(s) or guardian, a culturally sensitive program and teacher/professor, and an array of opportunities and choices. Based on the formula, $ES = F + S + O$; i.e., Educational Success = Family + Schools + Opportunities and vice versa.

Comprehensive Support Model (CSM)

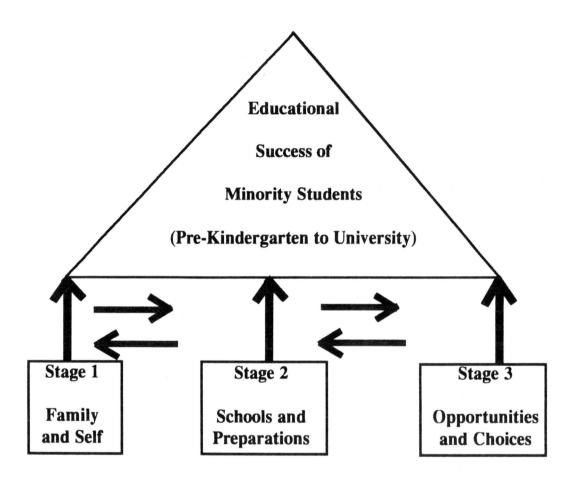

Educational

Success of

Minority Students

(Pre-Kindergarten to University)

Stage 1

Family
and Self

Stage 2

Schools and
Preparations

Stage 3

Opportunities
and Choices

Educational Success = Family + Schools + Opportunities
Formula: ES=F+S+O

Figure 8

There must be interactions between variables. The family must interact with schools, and schools must prepare the student for life so that he/she can take advantage of opportunities and choices. The CSM is multidimensional in nature - it respects intra-individual and inter-individual differences in all students. Evidently, the CSM is not a panacea, it is an antidote. We must be optimistic about what we learn, and we must continue to learn!

It is time we started listening actively to other voices--they might have useful prescriptions. For instance, conservative minority scholars and educators (like Dr. Glen Loury of Boston University and Dr. Walter Williams of George Mason University) must not be caricatured for their ideals. Minority and majority communities can learn from them. I am reminded of the African proverb that my father repeated many times when he tried to advise me to listen--this proverb states: "The fly without an advisor follows the cadaver into the grave." We can no longer afford to downplay their ideas on self-dignity, self-determination, self-respect and self-responsibility (D'Souza, 1991; Loury, 1985; Sowell, 1981; Washington, 1938; Williams, 1981). These ideas must be incorporated into multicultural education if we are to help minority students to make functional goal-directed decisions. I am not suggesting a wholesale consumption of their ideas--I am merely suggesting we incorporate ideas that enhance self-dignity of minorities into educational programs. As I indicated earlier, multicultural education must incorporate multidimensional ideas which will assist all individuals to maximize their potential and survive in today's complex society.

Finally, as teachers and service providers, our ethical and multicultural challenges must be our continuous zest to learn who we are and what we can do to make a difference. Logically, to make any remarkable difference, we must learn the facts when we are in doubt, we must change the ways we think, we must use resource persons when we lack the knowledge, we must build self-concepts and not destroy them, we must teach different students with different techniques, we must endeavor to make the right choices, and we must continue to learn (Obiakor, 1994). We have the option to light our candle or curse our darkness. We cannot afford to do the latter if we are really serious about multicultural education and relationships in our classrooms, schools and communities. Our future is bright. But, if we do nothing, it will be at stake. We only need to put the knowledge we have gained into practice. We must continue to learn how we can apply this knowledge to meet the unique needs of *all* our students.

Afterword

We often feel relieved and less deficient when we know others are
bothered by some of the same confusions that trouble us. That
makes it easier for us to accept ourselves, relax our anxieties, and
think rationally about what is or is not valuable. The sharing of
thoughts and impulses--especially when it is done in a supportive,
nonjudgmental climate--has the effect of freeing our intelligence.
(Harmin, 1977, p. 13)

I had talked with many of my friends and mentors (Whites and
minorities) about their writing this Afterword. They had accepted. Right about
the time I was deciding on who should write the Afterword, I was invited to do
the keynote speech for the Dr. Martin Luther King, Jr. Holiday Celebration
which was collaboratively organized by Emporia State University, Emporia's
Unified School District and the City of Emporia on January 17, 1994. It was
an excellent multicultural educational scene to see Anglo-Americans, African-
Americans, Asian-Americans, Hispanic-Americans, Native-Americans and
people of other nationalities marching together to an African-American Baptist
Church, the site of the celebration. All speakers (Whites and minorities) had
the same message, i.e., how we can make the United States and the world a
place where the human potential can be maximized. We all believe measurable
efforts have been made to unite the human race but that more multicultural
education is needed for us to benefit from these efforts.

There is no better Afterword for this book than the speech that I delivered
during this celebration. The title of my speech was "Going into the Mind's
Eyes of Dr. King: Surviving Today's Changing World." The contents of the
speech summarize the major thrust of this book. As we can see, I strongly
believe Dr. King's dreams are not dead. The problem today is that we have
stopped dreaming. We must go back to basics to understand the tenets of our
freedom and justice if we are to survive our changing world. The question is,
How can we understand our freedom and justice without multicultural learning
and teaching? As I indicated in many instances, multicultural education is not
just a "White thing" or a "Black thing"--it must be an "universal thing." Below
is this memorable speech:

Distinguished Guests, Ladies and Gentlemen! I thank the Almighty God
for giving me the health and life to deliver this speech. Three questions will
be explored in this presentation. They are: (1) Who was Dr. King? (2) What

legacies did he leave? (3) What are the impacts of his legacies on today's changing world?

Who was Dr. King?

Dr. King was a principled man who had the dream of redeeming mankind of bigotry, racism and hatred. He believed in nonviolent approaches to resolving these problems. In my 1990 book, *The Unseen Truth*, I wrote a poem titled, "The King's Mission" which highlighted the trials and tribulations of Dr. King.

A new king was born;
And Mike was his name.
He had the sincere devotion
To redeem mankind of bigotry
And to cleanse the world of racism.

Brilliant was the king
As Doctorate he earned at twenty-six
Atlanta was his Southern base
As he marched the streets
Of Birmingham and Selma.

The king sailed to India and Africa
Discovering the root of his drive
To crusade in Chicago and Florida
And to send the vivacious message
Of "I Have a Dream" in Washington.

The king dumbfounded the world
When at thirty-five Nobel Peace Prize he won
And his advocacy placidly created
The Civil Rights Act--
The pillar of freedom in America.

Viciously killed in Memphis was the king;
To fly a normal pitch at thirty-nine
He was nipped in the bud;
Still America celebrates his birthday

As his dream lives on.

Coretta Scott King (1983), in the book, *The Words of Martin Luther King, Jr.*, recounted memorable speeches of Dr. King. To enhance the sense of community amongst people, Dr. King indicated that "an individual has not started living until he (or she) can rise above the narrow confines of his (or her) individualistic concerns to the broader concerns of all humanity" (p. 17). On this same issue, he suggested:

> We must develop and maintain the capacity to forgive. He (or she) who is devoid of the power to forgive is devoid of the power to love. There is some good in the worst of us and some evil in the best of us. When we discover this, we are less prone to hate our enemies. (p. 23)

Also, on this same issue, he added:

> The ultimate measure of a man (or woman) is not where he (or she) stands in moments of comfort and convenience, but where he (or she) stands at trials of challenge and controversy. The true neighbor will risk his (or her) position, his (or her) prestige, and even his (or her) life for the welfare of others. In dangerous valleys and hazardous pathways, he (or she) will lift some bruised and beaten brother (or sister) to a higher and more noble life. (p. 24)

On the issue of racism, Dr. King warned that "there is little hope for us until we become tough-minded enough to break loose from the shackles of prejudice, half-truths and downright ignorance" (p. 30). In my 1991 book, *From the Heart*, I wrote a poem titled, "Holocaust (How Intelligent is Man?)" where I challenged the intelligence of human-beings who advocate hatred.

> How intelligent is man
> to support the holocaust
> that took the lives
> of many Jews?
>
> How intelligent is man
> to permit the killings
> that take place
> during wars?

How intelligent is man
to encourage the racism
that exists
in this world?

How intelligent is man
to allow anti-semitism
that flourishes
in many ways?

How intelligent is man
to permit the hatred
that ruins the lives
of other humans?

How intelligent is man
to encourage the slave mentality
that destroys creative tendencies
of other humans?

What Legacies did Dr. King Leave?

Even in his anguish, Dr. King left us legacies of civil rights, justice, freedom, faith and religion, nonviolence and peace. For example, on the issue of peace, Dr. King explained that "hatred and bitterness can never cure the disease of fear; ugly love can do that. Hatred paralyzes life; love releases it. Hatred confuses life; love harmonizes it. Hatred darkens life; love illumines it" (p. 90). In his "I Have a Dream" speech of August 28, 1963 in Washington D.C., Dr. King reaffirmed his wonderful legacies to the world when he stated:

...I say to you today, my friends, so even though we face the difficulties of today and tomorrow, I still have a dream. It is a dream deeply rooted in the American dream. I have a dream that one day this nation will rise up and live out the true meaning of its creed: "We hold these truths to be self-evident; that all men are created equal." . . . .
...And this will be the day. This will be the day when all of God's children will be able to sing with new meaning "My country 'tis of thee, sweet land of liberty, of thee I sing. Land where my fathers died, land of the pilgrim's pride, from every mountainside, let freedom ring." . . . . . .

...And when this happens, and when we allow freedom to ring, when we let it ring from every village and every hamlet, from every state and every city, we will be able to speed up that day when all of God's children, black men and white men, Jews and Gentiles, Protestants and Catholics, will be able to join hands and sing in the words of that old Negro spiritual, "Free at last! Free at last! Thank God Almighty, we are free at last!" (pp. 97-98)

Like Dr. King, I believe a bright future is possible for America and the World. We have seen numerous changes that have excited us. We now see opportunities and choices for peoples of different races, colors, genders, religions and national origins. Who would have dreamed that an African-American (retired General Colin Powell) who migrated to the United States with his parents from Jamaica, West Indies would become the Chairman of the Joint Chiefs of Staff of the United States Military? Who would have dreamed minorities would assume the kinds of positions they assume today in the corporate world and in colleges and universities? Who would have dreamed that an African-American (Governor Douglas Wilder) would be Governor of Virginia? Who would have dreamed that many of our cities would have Mayors who are African-Americans? Who would have dreamed that states like Kansas, New Jersey, Texas, etc. would have female Governors? Who would have dreamed that an African-American would have been elected a United States Senator from the State of Illinois? Who would have dreamed that a lady would be the President of Emporia's Chamber of Commerce? Who would have dreamed that the Berlin Wall dividing East and West Germany would fall? Who would have dreamed that an Israeli leader would shake hands of peace with a Palestinian Liberation Organization (PLO) leader? Who would have dreamed that South Africa will have a "one-man, one vote" election in 1994 with Nelson Mandela predicted to be the new President? Who would have dreamed that the daughter of Fidel Castro would seek political asylum in the United States? Many remarkable events have taken place. We cannot deny them.

What are the Impacts of His Legacies in Today's Changing World?

Our world is changing and our demographics are changing. Today, ethics, morality, spirituality, multiculturalism, inclusion and collaboration have become major issues. All issues are still politicized along racial lines, and we still search for *true peace*. Dr. King travelled far and wide to develop a philosophy that was deeply rooted in the American dream. He believed in excellence just as he believed in equality. Today, most people are running away from responsibilities. For instance, Whites blame Blacks, Blacks blame Whites, and no one is assuming responsibility. The progress we have seen today would have been impossible without the unity of all people. Dr. King will be crying in his grave when he sees the murder rates in our cities today. He will be dumbfounded to see the lack of spirituality, morality and ethics today. He will be very distressed to see Blacks killing Blacks and blaming Whites. He will be frustrated to see our "babies" having babies. He will be very angry to see the drug abuse and dealings taking place in America today. He will be upset to see many Americans relying on "welfares" and "affirmation action regulations" to survive. He will be distressed to see the self-hatred and total disregard for human life in America today. He will be rolling over in his grave to see that African-American Mayors are unable to stop the decay and killings in our inner-cities. He will be upset to see savage inequalities in school funding today. He will be frustrated to see that predominantly White colleges and universities are not making serious efforts to recruit, retain and promote minority students, faculty and staff. He will be wondering why separatism (and not inclusiveness) has become the order of the day. Finally, he will be frustrated with Democrats and Republicans--my hunch is that he will be an independent with a conservative slant. In other words, he will respect individuals for their productivity and not for their races, political affiliations and religious denominations.

Dr. King was quasi-optimistic before he was assassinated in Memphis, Tennessee on April 4, 1968. In his "I've Been to the Mountain Top" speech of April 3, 1968, Dr. King challenged us all when he stated:

> Let us rise up tonight with a greater readiness. Let us stand with a greater determination. And, let us move on in these powerful days, these days of challenge, to make America what it ought to be. We have an opportunity to make a better nation. And I want to thank God, once more, for allowing me to be here with you. ...I don't know what will happen now. We've got some difficult days ahead. But it really doesn't matter with me now, because I've been to the mountain top. And I don't mind. Like anybody, I would like to live a long life; longevity has its place. But I'm not concerned about that now. I just want to do God's will. And He's allowed me to go up to the mountain. And I've looked over. And I've seen the promised land. I may not get there with you. But I want you to know tonight that we as a people will get to the

promised land. And I'm happy tonight, I'm not worried about anything.
I'm not fearing any man. Mine eyes have seen the glory of the coming
of the Lord. (pp. 93-94)

Conclusion

Apparently, in Dr. King's optimism, we could see his skepticism, i.e., not
getting to the promised land with others. Today, it appears that we have
stopped dreaming. We ought to be worried about the growing underclass in
America. We were worried some years ago when the Soviet Union launched
the Sputnik. We were forced to dig deep into our creative instincts. Today,
we seem to be satisfied with mediocrity. We spend so much time categorizing
and labeling each other. We also spend so much time fearing the "unknown."
Inspite of all of these predicaments, the United States is still (and will
continue to be) the greatest country in the world. We must keep it that way.
We cannot afford to give up. We must learn to unite. We must stop blaming
all our ills on all White people or minorities. Let us begin to assume personal
responsibilities! Let us change our retrogressive ways for our world is
changing! Let us value and use our freedoms productively! Let us begin to
work together for our future is at stake! Let us continue to put our dreams into
practice! Let us continue to engage in self-knowledge, self-love,
self-empowerment, self-determination, self-responsibility and self-productivity!
Let us begin to enjoy and celebrate diversity for it is our strength! Let us
believe in "quality" for mediocrity is a dangerous phenomenon that has gone
beyond racial, cultural, color, gender and national boundaries!
Finally, let us continue to try our very best for life is what we make it!
My poem, "If We Try" sums it up (Obiakor, in press).

> If we try
> We might be free,
> If we try
> We might be happy,
> If we try
> We might be strong,
>
> If we try
> We might achieve,
> If we try
> We might overcome,

If we try
We might succeed.

Thank you and God's blessings!

References

Agada, J., & Obiakor, F.E. (1994, March). *The politics of education: Imperatives for African-American males in the 21st century.* Paper presented at the 22nd Annual National Association for Ethnic Studies (NAES) Conference, Kansas City, MO.

Algozzine, B. (1993). *50 simple ways to make teaching more fun.* Longmont, CO: Sopris West, Inc.

Algozzine, B., Maheady, L., Sacca, K. C., & O'Shea, D. (1990, April). Sometimes patent medicine works: A reply to Braaten, Kauffman, Braaten, Polsgrove, and Nelson. *Exceptional Children, 56*(6), 552-557.

Algozzine, B., & Obiakor, F. E. (in press). African-American quandaries in school programs. *Scholar and Educator.*

American Association of Colleges for Teacher Education. (1988). *Minority recruitment and retention: A public policy issue.* Washington, D.C.: Author.

Anderson, T. (1993). *Introduction to African-American studies.* Dubuque, IA: Kendall/Hunt Publishing Company.

Angelou, M. (1990). *I shall not be moved.* New York: Random House.

Anrig, G. R. (1985, May). Educational standards, testing, and equity. *Phi Delta Kappan, 66*(9), 623-625.

Arciniega, T. A. (1986). Cultural diversity in higher education: A critical continuing issue. In *Teaching to potential* (pp. 229-248). Las Cruces, NM: New Mexico State University.

Artiles, A., & Trent, S. (1994). Overrepresentation of minority students in special education: A continuing debate. *The Journal of Special Education, 27*(4), 410-437.

Asante, M. K. (1987). *The Afrocentric idea.* Philadelphia, PA: Temple University Press.

Atkinson, D. R., Morten, G., & Sue, D.W. (1993). *Counseling American minorities: A cross-cultural perspective (4th ed.).* Madison, WI: WCB Brown & Benchmark Publishers.

Ballenger, C. (1994, March). *The plight of Black students in public schools.* Unpublished essay.

Baer, G. L. (1991). *Turning our at-risk kids around.* Moravia, NY: Chronicle Guidance Publications, Inc.

Banks, J. A. (1977). *Multiethnic education: Practices and promises.* Bloomington, IN: Phi Delta Kappa Educational Foundation.

Banks, J. A. (1992). Multicultural education: Nature, challenges, and opportunities. In C. Diaz, *Multicultural education for the 21st century* (pp. 22-37). Washington, D.C.: National Education Association.

Banks, J. A. (1994). *An introduction to multicultural education.* Boston, MA: Allyn and Bacon.

Barker, N.C. (1993). The self and the Black male: Implications for school and society. In F. E. Obiakor and S. W. Stile, *Self-concept of exceptional learners: Current perspectives for educators* (pp. 168-183). Dubuque, IA: Kendall/Hunt Publishing Company.

Behrmann, J. (1991, Fall). Black students are at risk for low self-concept, but teachers can intervene to give youngsters the support they need. *Counterpoint, 12*(1), 21.

Bell, D. (1985). *And we are not saved: The elusive quest for racial justice.* New York: Basic books.

Bell, D. (1992). *Faces at the bottom of the well: The permanence of racism.* New York: Basic Books.

Binet, A. (1909). *Les idéas modernes sur les enfants (Modern ideas for children).* Paris, France: Flammarion.

Boyer, E. L. (1994, March 9). Creating the new American college. *The Chronicle of Higher Education,* p. A48.

Boyles, L. E. (1990, Fall). Collaboration and change. *Scholar and Educator, 14*(1), 9-14.

Bronowski, J. (1971). *The identity of man.* New York: American Museum Science Books.

Brooks, R. (1991). *The self-esteem teacher.* Circle Pines, MN: American Guidance Service.

Calabrese, R. L. (1989, Fall). Ethics: An educational priority. *Scholar and Educator, 13*(1), 32-40.

Canfield, J., & Wells, H. C. (1976). *100 ways to enhance self-concept in the classroom: A handbook for teachers and parents.* Englewood Cliffs, NJ: Prentice-Hall, Inc.

Castillo, G. (1974). *Left-handed teaching.* New York: Praefer.

Cohen, D. (1975). *Human nature, animal nature: The biology of human behavior.* New York: McGraw-Hill Book Co.

Curry, G. E. (1994, March). When being good isn't good enough. *Emerge,* p. 4.

Davis, W. E., & McCaul, E. J. (1990). *At-risk children and youth: A crisis in our schools and society.* Orono, ME: University of Maine.

DeBruyn, R. L. (1984, April 16). Upholding the tenets of education. *The Master Teacher, 15*(32), 1.

Della-Dora, D., & Blanchard, L. J. (1979). *Moving toward self-directed learning.* Alexandria, VA: Association for Supervision and Curriculum Development.

Dewey, J. (1958). *Philosophy of education.* Ames, IA: Littlefield, Adams & Co.

Dewey, J. (1960). *On experience, nature, and freedom.* Indianapolis, IN: The Bobbs-Merrill Company, Inc.

Diaz, C. (1992). *Multicultural education for the 21st century.* Washington D.C.: National Education Association Publication.

Dilworth, M. E. (1992). *Diversity in teacher education: New expectations.* San Francisco, CA: Jossey-Bass, Inc. Publishers.

D'Souza, D. (1991). *Illiberal education: The politics of race and sex on campus.* New York: Free Press.

DuBois, W. E. B. (1961). *The souls of the Black folk.* New York: Dodd, Mead & Company.

Emporia State University Project Partnership (1994). *Competencies, skills, and knowledge teacher education programs need to teach the inclusion teacher.* Emporia, KS: Author.

Fafunwa, A. B. (1976). *New perspectives in African education.* London, Britain: Macmillan Education Limited.

Feagin, J. R. (1978). *Racial and ethnic relations.* Englewood Cliffs, NJ: Prentice-Hall, Inc.

Frankl, V. E. (1984). *Man's search for meaning.* New York: Washington Square Press.

Franklin, J. H. (1980). *From slavery to freedom: A history of Negro Americans (5th ed.).* New York: Alfred A. Knopf.

Franklin, M. E. (1992, October/November). Culturally sensitive instructional practices for African-American learners with disabilities. *Exceptional Children, 59*(2), 115-122.

Garcia, E. (1994). *Understanding and meeting the challenge of student cultural diversity.* Boston, MA: Houghton Mifflin Company.

Garcia, R. L. (1992). Educating for human rights: A curriculum blueprint. In C. Diaz (Ed.), *Multicultural education for the 21st century* (pp. 166-178). Washington, D.C.: National Education Association Publication.

Gates, H. L. (1992). *Loose canons: Notes on the culture wars.* New York: Oxford University Press.

Gay, G. (1975, December). Organizing and designing curriculum. *Educational Leadership*, pp. 177-183.

Gay, G. (1992). Effective teaching practices for multicultural classrooms. In C. Diaz (Ed.), *Multicultural education for the 21st century* (pp. 38-56). Washington, D.C.: National Education Association Publication.

Glasser, W. (1986). *Control theory in the classroom.* New York: Harper & Row, Publishers.

Gollnich, D. M., & Chinn, P. C. (1990). *Multicultural education in a pluralistic society (3rd ed.).* New York: Merrill.

Goodlad, J. L. (1993). Access to knowledge. In J. L. Goodlad and T. C. Lovitt (Eds.), *Integrating general and special education* (pp. 1-22). New York: Merrill.

Gould, S. J. (1981). *The mismeasure of man.* New York: Norton.

Harmin, M. (1977). *What I've learned about values education.* Bloomington, IN: Phi Delta Kappa Education Foundation.

Harry, B. (1992). *Cultural diversity, families, and the special education system: Communication and empowerment.* New York: Columbia University Teachers College Press.

Harvey, W. B., & Scott-Jones, D. (1985, Summer). We can't find any: The elusiveness of Black faculty members in American higher education. *Issues in Education, 111*(1), 68-76.

Hill, H. D. (1989). *Effective strategies for teaching minority students.* Bloomington, IN: National Educational Service.

Hilliard, A. G. (1989, December). Cultural style in teaching and learning. *The Education Digest*, pp. 20-23.

Hilliard, A. G. (1992, October/November). The pitfalls and promises of special education practice. *Exceptional Children, 59*(2), 168-172.

Hilton, C. N. (1987). *Be my guest.* New York: Prentice Hall Press.

Jackson, J. L. (1988). In pursuit of equity, ethics, and excellence: The challenge to close the gap. In K. Ryan and J. M. Cooper (Eds.), *Kaleidoscope: Readings in education (5th ed.)* (pp. 444-448). Boston, MA: Houghton Mifflin Co.

Jenkins, A. H. (1982). *The psychology of the Afro-American: A humanistic approach.* New York: Pargamon Press.

Katz, P. A., & Taylor, D. A. (1988). *Eliminating racism: Profiles in controversy.* New York: Plenum Press.

King, C. S. (1983). *The words of Martin Luther King, Jr.* New York: Newmarket Press.

Kozol, J. (1991). *Savage inequalities: Children in American schools*. New York: Harper Perennial.

Kunjufu, J. (1984). *Developing positive self-images and discipline in Black children*. Chicago, IL: African-American Images.

Kuykendall, C. (1992). *From rage to hope: Strategies for reclaiming Black and Hispanic students*. Bloomington, IN: National Educational Service.

Loury, G. C. (1985, Spring). The moral quandary of the Black community. *The Public Interest, 79*, 9-22.

Lovitt, T. (1977). *In spite of my resistance . . . I've learned from children*. Columbus, OH: Charles E. Merrill Publishing Company.

Luhman, R., & Gilman, S. (1980). *Race and ethnic relations: The social and political experience of minority groups*. Belmont, CA: Wadsworth Publishing Company.

Magner, D. (1993). When Whites teach Black studies. *The Chronicle of Higher Education, 40*(15), A19.

Marable, M. (1990, February). Violence and crime in the Black community: Part two of a two part series. *Jackson Advocate, 51*(19), 5A.

Marable, M. (1993, October). Education and the promise of equality. *Jackson Advocate, 56*(3), 5A.

Matsumoto, D. (1994). *People: Psychology from a cultural perspective*. Pacific Grove, CA: Brooks/Cole Publishing Company.

Mayer, F. (1973). *Education for a new society*. Bloomington, IN: Phi Delta Kappa Education Foundation.

McWhirter, J. J., McWhirter, B. T., McWhirter, A. M., & McWhirter, E. H. (1993). *At-risk youth: A comprehensive response for counselors, teachers and human service professionals*. Pacific Grove, CA : Brooks/Cole Publishing Company.

Mickler, M. J. (1993). Academic self-concept: An exploration of traditions . In F. E. Obiakor and S. W. Stile, *Self-concept of exceptional learners: Current perspectives for educators* (pp. 113-147). Dubuque, IA: Kendall/Hunt Publishing Company.

Minton, H. L., & Schneider, F. W. (1980). *Differential psychology*. Prospect Heights, IL: Waveland Press, Inc.

Montagu, A. (1986). Foreword. In R. Benedict and G. Weltfish, *The races of mankind* (pp. 1-4). New York: Public Affairs Committee, Inc.

Moore, A. (1991, March 25). Need someone to blame? Just say a black man did it. *The Wichita Eagle*, p. 11A.

Mphahlele, E. (1974). *The African image*. New York: Praeger Publishers.

Myers, A. F., & Williams, C. O. (1954). *Education in a democracy (4th ed.).* New York: Prentice-Hall, Inc.

Nieto, S. (1992). *Affirming diversity: The sociopolitical context of multicultural education.* New York: Longman.

Nyerere, J. K. (1985). Education in Tanzania. *Harvard Educational Review, 55*(1), 45-52.

Obiakor, F. E. (1990). *The unseen truth: Collection of poems.* Chattanooga, TN: Damballah Press.

Obiakor, F. E. (1991). *From the heart.* Chattanooga, TN: Damballah Press.

Obiakor, F. E. (1992a). *The twisted faith.* Chattanooga, TN: Damballah Press.

Obiakor, F. E. (1992b, October/November). Self-concept of African-American students: An operational model for special education. *Exceptional Children, 59*(2), 160-167.

Obiakor, F. E. (1993). Opportunity and choice in higher education: Perspectives of African-American scholars. *SAEOPP Journal: Journal of the Southeastern Association of Educational Opportunity Program Personnel, 12*(2), 31-44.

Obiakor, F. E. (1994, February). *Valuing diversity: African-American culture, spirituality, morality, and value judgement.* Keynote Address during the Black History Month Celebration, Indiana University of Pennsylvania, Indiana, PA.

Obiakor, F. E. (in press). *The passage of time.* Chattanooga, TN: Damballah Press.

Obiakor, F. E., Algozzine, B., & Ford, B. A. (1993, October). Urban education, the General Education Initiative, and service delivery to African-American students. *Urban Education, 28*(3), 313-327.

Obiakor, F. E., & Barker, N. C. (1993, Winter). The politics of higher education: Perspectives for African-Americans in the 21st century. *The Western Journal of Black Studies, 17*(4), 219-226.

Obiakor, F. E., & Maltby, G. P. (1989). *Pragmatism and education in Africa: Handbook for educators and development planners.* Dubuque, IA: Kendall/Hunt Publishing Co.

Obiakor, F. E., Patton, J. M., & Ford, B. A. (Eds.) (1992, October/November). Special Issue: Issues in the education of African-American youth in special education settings. *Exceptional Children, 59*(2), 97-176.

Obiakor, F. E., & Stile, S. W. (1993). *Self-concept of exceptional learners: Current perspectives for educators.* Dubuque, IA: Kendall/Hunt Publishing Co.

Obiakor, F. E., Stile, S. W., & Muller, D. (1993). Self-concept in school programs: Conceptual and research foundations. In F. E. Obiakor and S. W. Stile, *Self-concept of exceptional learners: Current perspectives for educators (pp. 1-17).* Dubuque, IA: Kendall/Hunt Publishing Co.

O'Brien, S. J. (1991, Spring). How do you raise respectful children in a disrespectful world? *Childhood Education,* pp. 183-184.

Ogbu, J. U. (1978). *Minority education and caste.* San Francisco, CA: Academic Press.

Ogbu, J. U. (1988, Spring). Human intelligence testing: A cultural ecological perspective. *National Forum: The Phi Kappa Phi Journal, 68*(2), 23-29.

Ogbu, J. U. (1990, August). Understanding diversity: Summary statements. *Education and Urban Society, 22*(4), 425-429.

Ortiz, A. A., & Ramirez, B. A. (1989). *Schools and the culturally diverse exceptional student: Promising practices and future directions.* Reston, VA: The Council for Exceptional Children.

Owens, L. (1994, March 11). A personal letter to Dr. Festus Obiakor, Emporia State University, Emporia, Kansas.

Painter, N. I. (1994, March 23). It's time to acknowledge the damage inflicted by intolerance. *The Chronicle of Higher Education,* p. A64.

Pang, V. O. (1992). Institutional climate: Developing an effective multicultural school community. In C. Diaz (Ed.), *Multicultural education for the 21st century* (pp. 57-71). Washington, D.C.: National Education Association Publication.

Parillo, V. M. (1980). *Strangers to these shores: Race and ethnic relations in the United States.* Boston, MA: Houghton Mifflin Co.

Pearson, J. C., & Nelson, P. E. (1982). *Understanding and sharing: An introduction to speech communication (2nd ed.).* Dubuque, IA: Wm. C. Brown Company Publishers.

Pederson, P. B. (1991, September/October). Multiculturalism as a generic approach to counseling. *The Journal of Counseling and Development, 70*(1), 6-12.

Pett, J. (1993, June). *Pett Peeves.* Syndicated cartoon.

Pope, C. F. (1994, March 30). The challenges posed by radical Afrocentrism when a White professor teaches Black history. *The Chronicle of Higher Education,* pp. B1-B3.

Princes, C. (1994, March). *My experiences as director of a multicultural center.* Unpublished essay.

Rahija, J. E. (1993a, Fall). "Friends Forever." Unpublished poem.

Rahija, J. E. (1993b, Fall). "Happiness." Unpublished poem.

Roche, D. A. (1990). Saving the babies: The educator's role in preventing infant mortality. *Scholar and Educator, 13*(2), 29-33.

Samuda, R. J. (1975). *Psychological testing of American minorities: Issues and consequences.* New York: Harper & Row.

Samuda, R. J., & Lewis, J. (1992). Evaluation practices for the multicultural classroom. In C. Diaz (Ed.), *Multicultural education for the 21st century* (pp. 97-111). Washington, D.C.: National Education Association Publication.

Sauder, P. (1994, March 18). A letter to Dr. Festus Obiakor, Emporia State University, Emporia, Kansas.

Schlesinger, A. M. (1992). *The disuniting of America: Reflections on a multicultural society.* New York: W. W. Norton & Company.

Shade, B. R. (1989). *Culture, style, and the educative process.* Springfield, IL: Charles C. Thomas.

Sleeter, C. E. (1992). *Keepers of the American dream: A study of staff development and multicultural education.* London, England: The Falmer Press.

Sowell, T. (1981). *Ethnic America.* New York: Basic Books, Inc.

Spring, J. (1994). *Deculturalization and the struggle for equality: A brief history of the education of dominated cultures in the United States.* New York: McGraw-Hill, Inc.

Staples, R. (1984, March/April). Racial ideology and intellectual racism: Blacks in academia. *The Black Scholar,* pp. 2-17.

Steele, S. (1990a). *The content of our character.* New York: Harper Perennial.

Steele, S. (1990b, October 3). The "unseen agent" of low self-esteem. *Education Week,* p. 36.

Sullivan, K., Walko, A., & DiSibio, R. (1990, Spring). Quality, integrity and confusion: A view of the teaching profession. *Scholar and Educator, 13*(2), 67-78.

Toffler, A. (1982). *The third wave.* New York: Bantam Books.

Toffler, A. (1991). *Powershift.* New York: Bantam Books.

Washington, B. T. (1938). *Up from slavery.* New York: Doubleday.

Weaver, K. (1994, March). *Experiences of a peacecorper.* Unpublished essay.

Weikart, D. P. (1977). Preschool intervention for the disadvantaged child: A challenge for special education. In H. H. Spicker, M. J. Anastasiow and W. L. Hodges (Eds.), *Children with special needs: Early development and education* (pp. 73-89). Minneapolis, MN: Leadership Training Institute/Special Education, University of Minnesota.

Weintraub, D. (1993, September 29). A letter to Dr. Festus Obiakor, Emporia State University, Emporia, Kansas.

West, C. (1993). *Race matters*. New York: Vintage Books.

Williams, W. E. (1981). Inner city parents and freedom of choice. In *Black education and the inner city* (pp. 9-13). Washington, D.C.: The Lincoln Institute for Research and Education.

Woodson, C. G. (1933). *The mis-education of the Negro*. Philadelphia, PA: Hakim's Publications.

Ysseldyke, J. E., Algozzine, B., & Thurlow, M. L. (1992). *Critical issues in special education*. Boston, MA: Houghton Mifflin Company.